Praise for *Children At Promise*

"Tim Stuart and Cheryl Bostrom offer a unique and practical perspective on how to have a godly, eternal impact on children. Their message is especially critical to those young people whose lives have been characterized by disappointment and rejection."

—Dr. Bill Bright, founder, president, chairman emeritus, Campus Crusade for Christ

"Every child is bound to bump into tough times, and these experiences are sure to shape their character for good or ill. *Children At Promise* is an immensely practical and inspirational tool for helping kids rise above adversity—and succeed not only in spite of it, but because of it. This book is a winner!"

—Les Parrott, professor of clinical psychology, Seattle Pacific University; and author, *Helping Your Struggling Teenager*

"Teachers of every stripe, public and private, will benefit from *Children At Promise*. Taken seriously, it would revolutionize American education. Every prospective and practicing parent and teacher will want to read this book. I needed this thirty-five years ago when I started teaching, and before I became a principal and a parent."

—Ron Polinder, executive director, Rehoboth Christian School

"We've heard much from government in recent years about 'leaving no child behind.' In *Children At Promise*, Stuart and Bostrom show what it will take from the rest of us to make it happen, one child at a time."

—Dr. Duane Litfin, president, Wheaton College

"Tim Stuart and Cheryl Bostrom recognize that 100 percent of all children are at risk but that 100 percent are also 'At Promise.' This thinking could start a much-needed revolution. Brilliant work!"

—Marilyn Meberg, author and speaker, Women of Faith International

"*Children At Promise* uncovers an insightful and inspiring view of 'at-risk' children, a term that encompasses every child as they overcome everyday obstacles and 'grow and go' in God's love. This detailed account of the

effect of a mentor, backed by relevant scripture, is an outstanding refer-
ence and 'operating manual' for any faith-based mentoring program."
—Foster Friess, founder and chairman, Friess Associates; adviser to the
Brandywine Mutual Funds; and president, The Lynn and Foster Friess
Family Foundation

"*Children At Promise* promises real help to real parents and educators! This
book gives a new paradigm for looking at children that is biblically sound,
positive, and practical and, if followed, will turn children at risk into children of great promise."
—Claudia Arp and David Arp, authors, *Answering the Eight Cries of
the Spirited Child*

"Parents and educators who take the 'At Promise' paradigm seriously will
discover something new in themselves, something that they might not
have known was there. That 'something' is a sense of the positive potential in every child that, once we've come to believe in it and act on it,
changes each of us, one person at a time, in ways most miraculous."
—Dr. Arthur K. Ellis, professor and director, International Center for
Curriculum Studies, Seattle Pacific University.

"*Children At Promise* provides an important corrective to other formulas
for raising children, formulas that mistakenly assert that parents' most
important job is to protect their children from suffering. My children are
now older, but I wish I had heard this perspective when they were young."
—Tremper Longman, The Robert H. Gundry Professor of Biblical
Studies at Westmont College; and coauthor, *Bold Love* and
The Cry of the Soul

"*Children At Promise*" is very sound conceptually, covering a broad spec-
trum of crucial issues that develop a child's character. What a needed
word!"
—Dr. Les Carter, director of counseling at the Minirth Clinic; author
of *The Anger Trap*; and coauthor, *The Anger Workbook
for Christian Parents*

Children At Promise

9 Principles to Help Kids Thrive in an At-Risk World

Turning Hard Knocks into Opportunities for Success

Timothy S. Stuart and
Cheryl G. Bostrom

JOSSEY-BASS
A Wiley Imprint
www.josseybass.com

Published by Jossey-Bass
A Wiley Imprint
989 Market Street, San Francisco, CA 94103   www.josseybass.com

Jossey-Bass books and products are available through most bookstores. To contact Jossey-Bass directly, call our Customer Care Department within the United States at (800) 956-7739, outside the United States at (317) 572-3986, or fax to (317) 572-4002.

Jossey-Bass also publishes its books in a variety of electronic formats. Some content that appears in print may not be available in electronic books.

"At Promise" United States trademark registration by At Promise, Inc. pending.

Library of Congress Cataloging-in-Publication Data

Stuart, Timothy.
    Children at promise : 9 principles to help kids thrive in an at-risk world—turning hard knocks into opportunities for success / Timothy S. Stuart and Cheryl G. Bostrom.— 1st ed.
        p. cm.
    Includes bibliographical references.
    ISBN 0-7879-6875-7 (alk. paper)
    1. Problem children. 2. Church work with problem children. 3. Child rearing—Religious aspects—Christianity. I. Bostrom, Cheryl. II. Title.
BV4464.S78 2003
259'.2-dc21   2003010511

Printed in the United States of America
FIRST EDITION
HB Printing 10 9 8 7 6 5 4 3 2 1

Contents

Acknowledgments   ix

Introduction   1

Part One   The At-Promise Perspective   7

1. At Promise: A New Way of Thinking   9

2. The At-Risk World   21

3. Fear: Love's Counterfeit   33

Part Two   Requirements for Growth:
At-Promise Principles 1 and 2   47

4. Adversity and Pain Can Lead to Growth   49
    Principle 1: Adversity provides a catalyst for a child's
    character growth and is essential to success.

5. Trust Between a Caring Adult and a Child   69
    Principle 2: A trusting relationship with a caring adult
    helps a child interpret adversity and develop promise
    character.

Part Three   Promise Character: At-Promise Principles 3 to 9   89

6. Perseverance   91

  Principle 3: Perseverance empowers us to endure adversity and sustain hope.

7. Responsibility for Our Actions   101

  Principle 4: Responsibility for our actions keeps us from blaming others and teaches us that our choices have impact.

8. Optimism   113

  Principle 5: Optimism gives us lenses of hope through which we can see positive possibilities in the midst of pain.

9. Motivation from Identity   123

  Principle 6: Motivation from identity inspires us to live as individuals created in God's image, not as people labeled by our assets or deficits.

10. Integrity   135

  Principle 7: Integrity guides us to live honorably even when no one is looking and even when life hurts.

11. Service   143

  Principle 8: Service humbles us by shifting our attention away from ourselves and onto the needs of others.

12. Engaged Play   153

  Principle 9: Engaged play facilitates rest, healing, intimacy, and joy.

Conclusion   161

Study Guide: Conversation Starters   165

Notes   169

Recommended Reading   175

The Authors   179

For
Tyler, Moriah, and Ian Stuart
and
Andrew and Avery Bostrom

Our Children At Promise

Acknowledgments

Since its conception, so many people have contributed to this book! Our thanks here only begin to express our appreciation to Ed Solem for the countless hours of conversation and debate; Judy MacDonald for transcribing all those interviews; "the Weaklings" for accountability and prayer; Dr. Arthur Ellis for asking the hard and refining questions; Ken Sutton for truthful teaching; Chris Andrews and Betsey Cornwell for seeing the promise of the At Promise paradigm long before we did; Henry Algera, John Bond, and the rest of the Seattle Pacific University Doctoral Cohort Nine for helping birth this idea; the Bill and Melinda Gates Foundation for funding Tim's research; and Dr. Beth Blue Swadener for coining the thought-provoking and positive phrase At Promise.

We're especially grateful to the At-Promise team—Jim Janz, Jim Floor, Tim Leets, and Rod Janz—for believing in and modeling the At-Promise message every day. They have helped create a dream. We also thank our many friends and family members who listened, read, suggested, and prayed. Their encouragement has seen us through this project.

We have been privileged to work with editor Mark Kerr and his excellent team from Jossey-Bass. We thank them for their enthusiasm, professional excellence, and creative results. We couldn't have asked for a better experience. We also thank Linda Wagner for introducing us to the Jossey-Bass folks and for championing this book from the beginning.

We appreciate all of you who granted us interviews during our research. Although we could not include all of your stories in this book, every one of them contributed greatly to the development of the At-Promise paradigm. We thank Molly Yu-Chen Anderson, Andy Andrews, Laura Brisbane, Wayne Brisbane, Larry Burkett, Randy De Boer, Ruth Droullard, Don Eller, Lori Fransen, Ambassador John Hanford, Jerry Hobson, Jeff Jani, Dr. Tommy Lewis, Cindy Louws, Ambassador Tibor Nagy, Carol Ouellette, Bill and Karen Reinsma, Dr. Buffy Sainte-Marie, Dr. Robert Schuller, Darrell Smith, Sheldon Smith, Jan and Chris Soto, Debbie Stallcup, Judy Stankovich, Nancy Tupper, Ryan Walter, Dr. Deborah Wilds, Rev. Billy Zeoli, and those of you who asked to remain anonymous.

Many teachers and mentors have believed in us across the years. Some saw our promise long before we did. They are the kind of caring adults we write about here, the ones who help redefine and transform lives. They certainly have shaped ours. This book is a tribute to you, John and Sharon Aeschliman, Donna Cloud, Dr. George Durance, Grant Fiedler, Coach Foster, Gordy Hansen, Bev Herman, Ken Koeman, Dick Langum, Ken Lisk, Dr. Franklin Olson, Rod and Barbara Pence, Grey Pohl, Ron and Colleen Polinder, Father Pouliquain, Dr. Gordon and Doris Ripple, Dr. Cliff Schimmels, Marilyn Scribner, John and Pat Siemens, Dr. Walt and Pat Stuart, and Syd and Imogene Tozier.

And we remember the hundreds of young people who have inhabited our years and every corner of our lives. They continue to teach us, delight us, and humble us as we explore and develop their promise. We love them dearly.

Finally, we would like to thank our spouses. Blake, everything from your thoughtful evaluations of our manuscript to your unflagging support has blessed us immensely. And Mona, your fingerprints are on every page, your wisdom and heart in every concept.

Thank you.

June 2003
Lynden, Washington

Tim Stuart
Cheryl Bostrom

Introduction

Few things bring us more joy than catching glimpses of who our children are and who they are in the process of becoming. When my [Tim's] six-year-old daughter, Moriah Grace, defends her doll from a brotherly invasion, I see a picture of sheer promise! She will stand up to her brothers, oblivious to the odds against her. Outnumbered and outweighed two to one, she grabs the nearest hockey stick and fearlessly prepares for war. I suspect her feistiness resembles that of her pirate ancestor, Grace O'Malley (on her mother's side, of course!), who did battle off the coast of Ireland four hundred years ago. Moriah's protective nature opens a window for me into her spirit and paints a picture of the mother (or the professional hockey player) she may one day become.

Meanwhile Tyler, my eight-year-old, insists on bringing his field book along on our family outings to Whidbey Island so that he can meticulously insert his collected samples of nature. I can't help but smile as I peek into his mind and see the scientific discoveries he may someday make.

And when I see Ian, Moriah's twin brother, snuggle up on the couch and talk with his mother after she has read him a story, I think of the fortunate woman who someday will have this strong, gentle man to call her own.

As I [Cheryl] watch our son and daughter leave home for college, I review the wonderful traits my husband, Blake, and I have watched grow in them throughout their childhood. And I, like my colleague Tim, imagine ways those characteristics will play out in their future families, careers, and community lives. I see those kids as they have been, as they are now, and as my faith-tinted imagination sees their futures.

Our enthusiasm for children goes beyond our own families. Both of us have been educators, coaches, and mentors for many years and have completed graduate degrees (Tim, a doctorate in education; Cheryl, a master's degree) to better equip us to work with and on behalf of kids. I [Cheryl] have taught and coached students in grades 7–12 for multiple years, working with kids from ethnically diverse populations and with backgrounds that have varied from highly privileged to underprivileged. My husband and I have had dozens of children visit and stay in our home, some for short-term mentoring and others for longer-term foster care.

I [Tim] have served as a university professor as well as a secondary teacher and administrator for both advantaged and disadvantaged students in locations ranging from an exclusive Swiss boarding school to a Native American reservation. Spare time has found me coaching teams that varied in age and ability—from championship high school volleyball teams to first-grade Little League soccer.

Our mistakes and our successes in these remarkably different settings have convinced us of one thing: regardless of their backgrounds and whether they are in our homes, in the classroom, or on the playing field, the kids who share our lives need us to respond to them with meaningful, practical hope for their futures. Though it won't be easy, we want to view all children with joyful expectancy and to help them fulfill their deep potential.

But how? Some of the kids we have known seemed to have every advantage yet have not succeeded in using their opportunities well. Others have endured terrible trauma yet have overcome their victimization to contribute positively to their families and communities. Neither disadvantages nor advantages, neither risks nor protection from risks seem to be sole predictors of whether or not young people will grow up to make positive contributions to their societies.

Given those observations, I [Tim] was determined to learn more. Could I identify the combination of factors that gave kids the opportunity to succeed, regardless of their circumstances? Was there a common thread, a paradigm, that could apply to all young people? In a world with such disparate conditions, how and why could I legitimately hope that all children could have the opportunity to succeed? From these questions and from a phrase coined by Dr. Beth Blue Swadener in 1991, the At-Promise paradigm began to take shape in my mind.

As part of my work for Washington State University, I was teaching future educators at Northwest Indian College on the Lummi reservation when I ran across a statement by Swadener, recorded obscurely in a course syllabus. In an effort to deconstruct the label of *at risk* that had become so popular in educational circles, Dr. Swadener suggested: "Instead of seeing children and families as 'at risk,' all children and families might be viewed as 'at promise.'"[1]

Her words jumped off the page at me. Maybe they had such a profound effect because they stood in stark contrast to the prevailing at-risk vocabulary, exposing as incomplete a term that I really didn't want to believe in. Whatever the cause, when I heard the term *at promise*, I knew it captured the hope I had for my students. I liked it, so I started using it.

That summer as I led a team of international educators in Switzerland, I began using the term in an attempt to set a positive tone for the program. I wanted my teachers to see each and every student as At Promise. To my delight the phrase caught on. Later that summer two of the teachers on my team approached me and asked me to speak about identifying children as At Promise instead of at risk. They said that the idea moved them so much that they wanted me to share it with educators in San Antonio.

Positive feedback and interest at the Texas conference led me to conduct some informal research on *Children At Promise*. I started interviewing people I considered successful—not because they had attained the familiar measures of wealth, achievement, or popularity but because they were contributing positively to the moral and social fabric of their society.

When I asked these individuals what they considered the most important factors in their success, I expected one of their answers: they identified a relationship with an encouraging parent, mentor, or teacher as key. I was surprised, however, to hear a second recurring factor: they claimed that adversity helped them succeed! Until they underwent a powerful trial, they did not feel equipped to contribute positively to their world. They identified a lack of adversity as one of the risk factors that could have kept them from succeeding.

Before long I realized that for every one of those successful people, the ability to make those positive offerings had developed as the result of interplay between two influences: adversity and relationship. All respondents had experienced significant levels of adversity, and all had at least one person in their lives who believed in them, encouraged them, and urged them to achieve beyond what they thought was possible.

From this beginning *Children At Promise* was born. I later expanded my research to support a doctoral dissertation on this topic, which statistically examined the correlation between relationship and the ability of a child to perceive the benefits of adversity. And I asked coauthor Cheryl Bostrom to collaborate with me on this book. Her experience as an educator, writer, mentor, and parent; her background in psychology; and her commitment (like mine) to biblical truth brought ideas and support to the project that expanded and further validated the At-Promise paradigm. Together, we hope to communicate the At-Promise concept to parents and educators, as well as to men and women everywhere who mentor young people.

With that goal in mind, we offer readers this book. In Chapters One to Three, we explain the At-Promise paradigm and show how it offers a truer, more hopeful way of thinking about children than at-risk thinking. As part of that explanation, we introduce the AT-PROMISE acronym, which will help readers remember each of the foundational elements of At-Promise thinking. In Chapters Four and Five, which cover the AT portion of the acronym, we explain how a combination of *adversity* and a relationship of *trust* with an adult is necessary to a child's success. In Chapters Six through Twelve, we explore the seven character traits referred to by the letters PROMISE: *perseverance, responsibility, optimism, motivation, integrity, service,* and *engaged play.* Theory and practice have demonstrated how each of those traits contributes to a child's ability to succeed. These seven chapters examine the interplay between these distinct traits, the principles behind them, their place in the At-Promise paradigm, and their necessity for both children and adults.

We hope these insights encourage and direct others as much as they have us.

Part One

The At-Promise Perspective

Chapter One

At Promise: A New Way of Thinking

> You have to do your own growing no matter how
> tall your grandfather was.
>
> —*Abraham Lincoln*

Over coffee Larry reluctantly began telling his story. "I don't know why you want to interview me. I don't have any fuzzy stories to tell you about my youth. I barely had a childhood."

He continued:

I was number five of eight children. My parents came through the Great Depression, which left an indelible imprint on their lives. . . . My father never got over the fact that he lost everything, so the rest of his life was dedicated to working. He was an electrician, a smart guy for sure, but he spent the rest of his life working himself to death. And that is what he thought the role of a father was. And my mother . . . never really liked kids, I guess . . . never put any time into her kids. So [my parents] didn't have much positive influence in my life . . . hadn't steered me in any particular direction.

"So what was the turning point?" we asked. The question surprised him. He looked at us as if we had caught him off guard. Then he said:

I remember [a defining] moment in my life. I was going into tenth grade. Up to that point, all through elementary school and early junior high and high school, I had heard the same thing from everybody: "As intelligent as you are, you ought to be able to make good grades—but you just don't try very hard." When football and baseball seasons would come around, I would raise my grades high enough to stay eligible. But beyond that, I would make D-minus, just enough not to fail.

I had an algebra teacher named Dan Blackwell who asked me to meet him after school. And he said to me, "Larry, obviously you have the ability to do this math, but you don't work at anything or apply any effort." Then he said, "I'll tell you what I am going to do. If you come into my room for one hour, two days a week after school, I'll help you catch up on your algebra." And he did. I met with him for the entire semester, almost half a year, twice a week after school for an hour. And he tutored me in math. It was the first time that anyone, any adult, had taken any interest in me whatsoever. He encouraged me, and we got to be very good friends. [With his help, I] raised my algebra scores from a D-minus to an A. Because I had learned that I could achieve, it changed my whole perspective.

From that point on, I don't know that I made anything less than an A in any subject. It took a lot to catch up, obviously, but otherwise I would have never been able to go to college. It wasn't a large amount of time [that Dan spent with me] when you think about it; he probably invested fifty hours in me, but [that relationship] just changed the direction of my whole life.

Larry's story isn't unusual. Millions of individuals could tell you their own versions, demonstrating again and again how adversity and relationship interact in people's lives to propel them toward meaningful success. Larry's experience, like that of so many others, exemplifies our premise that behind every truly successful individual is an At-Promise story: a story that involves adversity and at least one caring adult who participates in a child's life.

An Overview

What is an At-Promise story? This chapter contains the At-Promise paradigm in a nutshell. Here we summarize the need to replace at-risk thinking with a hopeful new mind-set and vocabulary, and we present At-Promise principles that answer that need. In later chapters we'll explain both the need for this paradigm shift and the principles one by one. Because the AT-PROMISE acronym outlined in this chapter gives you a road map connecting each principle, we recommend that you refer to these pages regularly.

Success Defined

Perhaps you read our opening story and said to yourself, "Well, Larry's teacher wouldn't have had the same effect on me. I wasn't bright like he was. No amount of tutoring or encouragement would have raised my grades to an A average. I'd have been glad to earn C's. You can't tell me that adversity and relationship give everybody a shot at success." You're right. Some definitions of success exclude us. Not everyone can earn A's. Nor will all of us be wealthy, talented, beautiful, powerful, or famous.

But what if we defined success differently? Is there a true, meaningful success that everyone can attain? At-Promise thinking depends on just such a definition. Therefore, from this point on, *to succeed* means to contribute positively to the moral and social fabric of society. That society consists of the communities (family, neighborhood, city, state, country, and world) in which we live. We believe this sort of success results from the development of character that can be produced when we positively interpret adversity in the context of a trusted relationship.

Larry succeeded not because of high grades or his athletic prowess but because he eventually used the lessons he learned through his painful childhood and through his relationship with Dan Blackwell. With Dan, Larry was learning more than how to achieve. He was learning to care by being cared for. Eventually, he used his skills to help families get out of debt. Today he has committed his resources to teaching people to manage their money wisely so that they can have more time and resources for things that matter—like relationships and helping others.

Has Larry Burkett succeeded? We think so, but not because he's well known as an author and radio host. Larry has succeeded by contributing to the moral and social well-being of others, including those who listen to his broadcasts and learn from his books.

This sort of success is available to every child who experiences both adversity and wise, caring, trusted relationship. Every child has the potential, the innate promise to know the success that comes from helping others. Although we cannot guarantee that a child will choose success, we can have unquenchable hope for every child we mentor, because once a child has both relationship and adversity, true success is available to that child, should he or she choose it.

Your At-Promise Story

Each person's life is marked in one way or another by relationship and adversity. Some grow up in relatively supportive, caring, and healthy environments; others recall childhoods devoid of support and blistered by difficult, adverse, or even abusive experiences. Many fall somewhere in the middle, knowing a good dose of both love and pain in varying degrees over a lifetime. Regardless of where we fall on this continuum, the intersecting points between our challenging circumstances and a positive, interactive relationship with someone who cared for us serve as catalysts for character growth in our lives. That character is foundational to true success.

As we saw with Larry, successful individuals who grew up in adverse situations inevitably point to a caring relationship as the key to their eventual success. On the other hand, successful individuals who grew up in nurturing and supportive environments point to the introduction of adversity in their lives as a key to their success.

We challenge you to take a look at your own life to see if this is true for you. If your childhood was more characterized by nurturing relationship, then we suspect that times of significant growth occurred when you encountered and dealt with difficulty. If your childhood was more characterized by pain and adversity, then we suspect that your turning point resulted from someone stepping into your life at a particularly difficult time, believing in you, and offering you hope. This has certainly been the case for us.

A New Paradigm

As a society we often believe that we must avoid adversity. We have seen how pain can damage kids, and we recognize family and cultural upheaval that both spawns and results from pain-inducing choices or circumstances. Therefore, we erroneously believe that all pain is bad and that if we want our children to succeed, we must shelter them from it. Sometimes we consciously decide this. Other times, although we may intellectually acknowledge adversity's usefulness, we still subconsciously try to shield children from the discomfort of trials.

Regularly we try to protect them in two ways. If we're advantaged enough, we shower them with material or circumstantial provisions. We think that if they just have enough stuff or opportunities, they'll be able to dodge much of life's pain. Similarly, many educators, social services personnel, and parents call for more programs—which may not be based on trusting relationships—to protect children from the adversity of this world.

Adversity scares us! But when we give in to fear-based thinking, we attempt to protect our children from pain through either provisions or programs. Fear causes us to place our children on an enormous life-support system that hooks kids up to a complex network of either stuff or programs as though their very breath depended on them. We fear that without these support structures, our children cannot survive. There is one problem with this thinking: our children do not need a complicated life-support system; they need us!

The At-Promise perspective is a 180-degree shift from fear-based thinking that places a higher priority on provisions and programs than on people. It suggests that we need to develop trusting relationships with children that can help them interpret adversity and use it as a building block for success. The At-Promise paradigm suggests that just as God uses adversity and relationships to mold and shape us, He also requires adversity and relationships to shape a child's success. That's right! We and the children we care about need both adversity and relationships if we are to experience more of our potential.

The Real State of Affairs

Our young people live in an imperfect, risk-laden world. At some point they will face people and circumstances that will mislead, discourage, hurt, harm, frighten, anger, defeat, or even victimize them, conceivably damaging their potential for future success. As much as we parents would like to, we cannot protect them from every possible pain, nor would we be wise to do so, because adversity is necessary to a child's growth.

The At-Promise Paradigm Offers Deep Hope

On one hand, At-Promise thinking recognizes the fact that each and every child arrives in this world equipped with a flawed nature, a nature that sometimes will be attracted to unhealthy thinking and behavior. Anyone who has worked or lived with children would agree with journalist and author G. K. Chesterton, who asserts that original sin is the one observable Christian doctrine.[1] Every child is indeed at risk and living in an at-risk world.

On the other hand, the At-Promise viewpoint finds its foundation in God's design for life—and for those kids both He and we care about. "'For I know the plans I have for you,' declares the Lord, 'plans to prosper you and not to harm you, plans to give you hope and a future'" (Jeremiah 29:11). He has good things in store for his children, even if they must go through pain to reach them. God will shape every kind of adversity—whether mild or horrible—into something beneficial for personal and communal growth, if we, in love, trust Him to show us the route to that growth.

How? We choose to trust God to use the adversity we have endured to nurture our own promise character. Then we—with His direction and power—do our best to help young people do the same thing. Although we certainly can't accomplish the transformation of behavior and circumstances in our own strength, God can. Romans 5:3–5 explains the pathway: ". . . we also rejoice in our sufferings, because we know that suffering produces perseverance; perseverance, character; and character, hope. And hope does not disappoint . . . us." This doesn't mean we like the suffering itself, but it does mean that no matter how terrible the painful circumstance and no matter how long we have to wait, we can endure the pain and the delay because hope and success can eventually emerge from it.

This is a difficult concept to accept without a framework of faith. No amount of theory or research can convince us to sustain unqualified hope for children. Without faith, we will encounter a point of pain beyond which we are humanly incapable of hoping. At that point, without a formula that always works, we will give up on the children we care about.

Fortunately, At-Promise thinking is not a guaranteed formula. It's better. It is a set of loving, faith-based principles supported by educational and psychological theory and research. It relies on the fact that we have a God who loves us, loves our children, and absolutely wants them to succeed. Fortunately, we do not have final say over the effectiveness of our mentoring. Fortunately, God's reach, capability, and control extend beyond our own, and ultimately it is He who interacts with our children, on a timetable far different from ours. He understands their free will far better than we do. And He absolutely reassures us that we are not in control; He is.

Even so, God invites us to participate in extracting our children's promise. We can apply principles He has taught us to help the children we care about learn to choose behaviors and attitudes that can lead to success. Remember, our definition of success does not include financial wealth or widespread influence. Instead, we can help children develop the character that will compel them to contribute positively to the moral and social fabric of society.

So we choose to acknowledge the risks our children address as imperfect people in an imperfect world, then to redirect our attention to their promise, an identity that defines them more accurately than does any potential risk. We choose to affirm the perspective that acknowledges the at-risk nature of children and yet still declares every child At Promise.

Importantly, kids' risk and their promise are not equally weighted. Because we believe that our children are designed to resemble their Creator, we have confidence in their varying degrees of ability to think, make decisions, understand good and bad, remember the past, envision the future, and love. Because they are made in God's image, they have the powerful capacity for developing character like His, whether they are brilliant or mentally handicapped, athletic or palsied, emotionally secure or traumatized. That gives us hope in their capability to overcome and grow through difficulty.

God offers all children the power to rise above adversity and succeed not only in spite of it but because of it. To the degree to which they are receptive, He works within them, using all of life's past, present, and future experiences and relationships—particularly the painful ones—to build character and success. We know that their promise is more indomitable than any challenges they may encounter.

When we concentrate on the promise in children and show them how to unfold it, the potential pain-causing hazards in their world can become character-building agents. According to Drs. Lawrence Calhoun and Richard Tedeschi, who coined the term and extensively researched the concept of *posttraumatic growth*, such growth "is set in motion by the same sets of events that produce psychological distress and that can also place the individual at increased risk of psychological difficulties. . . . The trauma

typically leads to a questioning and reevaluation of many important assumptions previously held . . . we see both distress and
growth coexisting in persons in the aftermath of trauma."[2] Therefore, instead of expecting children to fall unless we keep pain away,
we expect children to encounter life's adversity, then expect them
to grow and succeed because of it. Why? Because we will travel
with them and show them the way.

Nine Interacting Principles

For twelve months we interviewed many people in an attempt to
fully develop trustworthy At-Promise principles. During these
interviews we asked individuals from a wide range of backgrounds
to identify key factors that contributed to their success. Some of
these people are highly visible; others are known only in their
immediate communities. All, however, fit our definition of *successful*. The results of these interviews yielded recurring themes now
captured in the nine At-Promise principles, which form the foundation for this book.

The acronym AT-PROMISE can help readers remember these
key principles, giving them staying power as we learn to apply them
to our relationships with young people. Two overarching principles
are represented by the acronym's first two letters:

A *Adversity* provides a catalyst for a child's character growth
   and is essential to success.

T A *trusting relationship* with a caring adult helps a child
   interpret adversity and develop promise character.

These two elements—adversity and a trusting relationship—interact with each other to create a fertile environment critical for a
child's positive growth and development. Children are better
equipped for successful, life-enhancing growth when they experience difficult trials in the context of a meaningful relationship
with a caring adult.

The remaining seven principles represent the character traits that grow out of the intersection of adversity and trusted relationship in the child's life. Each of these principles can contribute powerfully to a child's ability to succeed. We can remember them with the PROMISE portion of the acronym:

P   *Perseverance* empowers us to endure adversity and sustain hope.

R   *Responsibility for our actions* keeps us from blaming others and teaches us that our choices have impact.

O   *Optimism* gives us lenses of hope through which we can see positive possibilities in the midst of pain.

M   *Motivation from identity* inspires us to live as individuals created in God's image, not as people labeled by our assets or deficits.

I   *Integrity* guides us to live honorably even when no one is looking and even when life hurts.

S   *Service* humbles us by shifting our attention away from ourselves and onto the needs of others.

E   *Engaged play* facilitates rest, healing, intimacy, and joy.

Without a caring adult, a child can be quickly overwhelmed by adversity. Without adversity, a caring relationship can indulge a child. Without developing components of a promise character, a child will not have the training to succeed. The absence of any of these principles—adversity, trusted relationship, or promise character—can delay maturation of a child's potential.

What Can We Do?

The degree to which our children develop these traits will largely depend upon three factors within our control:

- The time a caring adult spends building trust with a child
- The number of promise character traits the adult can offer a child
- The way the caring adult chooses to interpret adversity to the child

The more time we can spend with a young person, the more time we have to build a trusted influence with that child. The more character we are cultivating, the more we can model character and offer wise counsel to that child.

We can't control, however, the ultimate tenderness or resistance of a child—either to a caring adult or to God's truth. In ways beyond our understanding, God allows each of us the freedom to trust Him and learn from Him or to mistrust Him and refuse His instruction.

Nor can we control God's timing. Loaves of truth we place within a young heart may not finish cooking for twenty years or more! Just because we don't see positive results from our time spent with kids, doesn't mean they aren't rising in that oven. They may take decades of adversity's heat to finish baking.

Helping children grow exhilarates. It also hurts. We know both the joy and the pain as we live, work, play, and wait alongside the young people in each of our families. For both the Stuart and Bostrom children, who range in age from six to twenty, adversity is a fact of life. Even as we write this, we hurt with and for and because of our children. That hurting is part of growth, both theirs and ours, as we help our kids climb toward the fulfillment of their incredible promise.

A Call to Action

The At-Promise perspective is a practical, trustworthy, and hope-filled approach to fulfilling the deepest promise in children. This perspective applies to all kids, ranging from those who are preschool-aged, home-schooled, or attending small private schools; to those who are enrolled in large school systems, attend college, or have already completed their formal education. It is a call to action and a vaccination against both hopelessness and an "epidemic of pessimism" among young people that Dr. Martin Seligman identifies in his book *The Optimistic Child*.[3]

At-Promise thinking articulates a mind-set for seeing past pain to hope, as well as a framework for evaluating our own impact on and responsibility to the young people in our lives. This mandate asks each caring adult to step forward and to invest deliberately in the life of a child.

What are our children really up against? Let's begin by looking at the risks that bombard them.

Remember . . .

- Behind every truly successful individual is an At-Promise story: a story that involves trials, adversity, and at least one caring adult who participates in a child's life.

- From this point on, *to succeed* means to contribute positively to the moral and social fabric of society.

- When we concentrate on the promise in children and show them how to unfold it, the potential pain-causing hazards in their world can become character-building agents.

Chapter Two

The At-Risk World

There is no pit so deep that He is not deeper still!
—*Corrie ten Boom*

More than once over the years, I [Cheryl] have fallen into the trap of predicting disaster based on my children's escapades. Though it happened years ago, I remember one situation all too clearly. Our preschool son, in retaliation for some squabble with his younger sister, deliberately put her tricycle under the rear wheels of my car and then hid in the orchard to watch me back over it. Sure enough, as soon as I backed out of the driveway, my right rear wheel mangled her little trike.

If I hadn't overreacted, I probably would have weighed my options immediately and then chosen a calmer response. The scene could have looked like this: Mom backs car over tricycle, placed behind tires by naughty little boy. Mom reviews circumstances and decides to see past his roughneck behavior to a brighter future. She discusses incident with boy and dispenses appropriate discipline. Boy, repentant, apologizes, pays for trike out of piggy bank, and says he'll never do anything like that again. Lesson learned, boy changed . . . a little bit.

Sometimes I'm just not that placid. When I first realized that this was no accident, that our son had planned that tricycle's destruction, I was shocked—and angry. "What in the world are you *doing?*" I howled at him. As I screeched, he hightailed it from behind a tree toward his bedroom—a very good destination, considering his mother's hostile state.

In retrospect I think fear fueled my anger. The premeditated nastiness of his act frightened me. Who was this young criminal? My imagination roared ahead to his teenage years, and I saw him slashing car tires . . . or worse. My beliefs about what his behavior meant shaped both the direction and intensity of my reaction. When I let my thoughts follow my fear, I labeled him and branded his future. But only briefly, I'm glad to say. Even so, ten minutes with a mom who was angrily reacting out of fear had driven the child to tears. What if I hadn't calmed down and then appropriately disciplined him? Where could fear have taken us?

Though our young son misbehaved, his action did not predict his future. Now twenty years old, he is compassionate and kind—and is developing deep, consistent promise character.

Promise Shrinks Risk's Power

Clearly, we see both promise and risk in our children. As parents or educators who love them, we view their quirks, their gestures, their reactions to circumstances, and their interactions with joyful anticipation, even as we recognize their need for discipline and instruction.

But fear can distort how we picture our children. If we fear for them, we may not objectively recognize their vulnerabilities but may instead project their current shortcomings onto the screen of their futures—as negative prophecies fulfilled. For example, when we learn that four-year-old Jacob stole candy at the grocery store today, we find ourselves imagining the child as a sullen, shoplifting teen tomorrow. When we bring home a shoplifting teen from the police station, our shattered trust may lead us to say to ourselves (or others), "She'll never amount to anything!" A typically self-centered teenage son may hear us say, "Unless you change, you'll be headed for divorce someday." When we learn that fifteen-year-old Brandon has been accessing Internet porn sites, we fear that sexual addiction lurks in his future. Our faulty, fearful thinking may prompt us to behave in ways that say, "We believe you'll fail."

Such thinking reflects the belief that children can't overcome risks. It also tells us that no one will be able to guide them safely.

Wrong! Risks are everywhere, certainly—and we do need to be aware of them—but we should refuse to surrender to them and refuse to allow them to paralyze us with fear.

Responding to Risk

In this chapter we will look at some of the obvious and hidden risks challenging our children today, as well as three common responses to them: labeling, denial, and fear. We will examine both the *at-risk* and *advantaged* labels ascribed to children, labels that are typically based on the degree of adversity or support these kids have experienced and that categorize our kids' propensity for success based on their assets and deficits, according to their environmental and intrinsic attributes. Then we will offer the At-Promise perspective as a loving alternative to those incomplete and inaccurate ways of thinking about and responding to young people.

At Risk of What?

In recent years the at-risk child has captured tremendous attention. Challenges affecting the lives of today's children have caused many researchers, politicians, and government agencies to identify 90 percent of U.S. children as at risk. This means that 90 percent of our children fit statistical profiles that put them at risk for some sort of failure. Such statistics tell us that nine out of ten kids on any playground, ninety out of one hundred teens in your daughter's school cafeteria, and 90 percent of the kids any of us know are at risk. According to some researchers, children who live with one or a combination of risk factors have an increased likelihood of failure in marriage, parenting, business, self-perception, or any of a dozen additional areas that many believe necessary to function competently in society.[1]

Although this data is daunting enough, we believe that the number of at-risk young people is even higher than 90 percent. When we line up all the threats to children, we can identify fully

100 percent of all kids as at risk for failure. Why 100 percent? Read on.

Familiar Risk Factors

Children deal with compound risks every day, dished up in a growing number of categories. You may recognize them: Emily, whose parents make minimum wage and get groceries at the food bank; Lilia, who arrived in this country two years ago and is just learning English; Philip, with attention deficit disorder; hyperactive Brett; Shannon, with epileptic seizures; and Tran, who fights depression. Alisa stayed in the hospital for months after her premature birth. Sam's parents treat him cruelly, and Marianna's mother died last year. Kate smokes marijuana daily, and fifteen-year-old Kim is pregnant. Liz finally joined the neighborhood gang that had been pressuring her. Joe? He comes home to an empty house. All these young people are statistically considered at risk in America today.

In addition, children are also called at risk if they have parents who dropped out of school; are very young; are divorced, remarried, or never married; have felony convictions; are in jail; or depend upon drugs or alcohol.

The numbers are staggering, even when one considers only a couple of the risk factors we've named. For example, in 1998 an astounding 2.8 million cases of potential child abuse were reported to the Child Protective Services.[2] In 1999 nearly 485,000 babies were born to teenage girls in the United States, with the vast majority of births occurring outside of marriage.[3]

Advantaged Kids Face Risks Too

"But those situations don't apply to my kid," you may reply. "I'm a pretty good parent. I have nurtured my children and have given them good educational opportunities, church upbringing, clothing, shelter, support. They are usually healthy, and I have protected them from pain."

Fair enough. But other factors can also throw a child into a tailspin. Indicators for risk go beyond the usual ones we've mentioned. Although the typical risk markers do not include a young person's high intelligence, strong talent, supportive environment, or educational or financial privileges, we suggest that experiencing those advantages without the benefit of interpreted adversity can pose serious risks to kids. These children run the risk of failing to fulfill their most meaningful potential, their deepest promise.

Statistically, advantaged children may be more likely to graduate from high school, go to college, and land high-paying jobs.[4] But will they truly have succeeded? Will they have developed the character traits that go hand in hand with making positive contributions to their communities' moral and social makeup?

When we pretend that advantages alone empower kids to succeed, we are in denial. Because we can see denial much more easily in others than in ourselves, let's take a look at Kyle, who lives in an upper-middle-class suburb. He's a starter on the football and basketball teams, and he gets pretty good grades. His well-meaning parents have protected him from pain—even the pain of hard work—to the best of their ability. Achievement has come easily to him; he hasn't suffered much. His parents are busy working to sustain the material comfort they all enjoy and are often too distracted to help him deal with trials he may encounter at school or in relationships or to challenge him on character issues. Like many parents of good kids, they assume that Kyle will succeed. After all, he has all the advantages, all the "provisions."

His teachers have done the same thing, often letting Kyle get away with unacceptable behavior or performance without holding him accountable for his actions, just as many teachers do for advantaged kids in your town and ours. Studies have shown that when teachers expect strong performance, they are more likely to inflate the grades of children they perceive as advantaged, capable kids.[5]

To make matters worse, if those children do not earn strong grades, many supportive parents will challenge teachers not to be so unreasonable in their grading practices. After all, lower grades hurt their kids' chances of getting into the good colleges!

Consequently, Kyle is at risk in an unexpected way: he has largely missed out on experiencing the adversity of natural consequences alongside a trusted adult who could help him evaluate it and grow stronger because of it. He too has a potential for failure in relationships and society.

Last year Kyle quit the track team because he wasn't winning races. (Never mind that he only gave minimal effort at turnouts.) He refused to register for a college preparatory English class because it was too much work. He got a few answers for the biology test from his girlfriend, who is in the class a period before his. (He forgot her birthday last week, but, hey, she'll get over it.) At Christmas dinner he barely acknowledged his grandmother, whom he sees three or four times a year. If his parents were watching for true success, they would instead see incipient signs of the observation in Proverbs 29:15: "Correction imparts wisdom, but a child left to itself disgraces his mother." They would spot his limited perseverance, his compromised integrity.

And what about children who may never learn to contend with adversity and who are handed everything—new cars, clothes, vacations, money? This scenario transcends socioeconomic groups, because many families go deeply in debt to make sure that their kids have all the material provisions money can buy. Such indulgences can actually put these advantaged children at risk. Like Kyle, pampered children run the risk of a self-indulgent lifestyle that leaves them with flabby character. Their self-absorption may limit or even prevent them from contributing positively to the moral and social fabric of their relationships and society. According to our definition of success, these kids risk falling short of their potential for true success.

Without the adversity that a trusted adult helps a child understand, a child can turn most anything—positive or negative—into a stumbling block to success. Even the wonderful opportunities we parents see as rich gifts can actually encumber children, who can misinterpret any situation and make destructive decisions in response.

All Kids Face Risks

"Wait a minute," we hear you say. "You really are calling just about every kid at risk." Yep. And here's one more item for the list: also at risk are children who make mistakes. Mess up. Sin. Every child will at some point disobey, disappoint, or rebel. All kids are born with a fallen nature and a free will. Not one child is exempt from this ultimate, deadly risk factor. We simply can't escape the fact that 100 percent of all children are at risk. We must allow that truth into our view. But if we are to help kids realize their promise, we must refuse to let risk factors devastate the landscape with negative labels.

Negative Labels

Many folks, spurred on by the educational system, do more than just recognize risk. They go one step further and label privileged children as advantaged and disadvantaged children as at risk. Then they voice those labels to themselves, to other adults, and even to the kids themselves, making them static and permanent. Like tattoos, labels mark young people. They don't wash off, and they are constant reminders of how we perceive them.

If labeling can mislead us, why do it? Why do we glue a label to traditionally identified at-risk kids that says, "Uh-oh. You're headed for trouble," even if they haven't gotten in trouble? Why do we label advantaged kids with the assumption "You're bound for success" even if they are morally headed the other direction?

Drs. James and Cherry Banks, professors of education at the University of Washington, identify a few worthwhile reasons to label but only if the labels are accurate. First, categorizing and labeling kids can help professionals communicate with others and evaluate research findings. Labeling can also allow advocacy groups (for example, parents of children with autism) to promote programs and spur legislative action, and they can make the special needs of exceptional children more visible.[6] Most significantly, accurate labeling can spot distinctions in learning or behavior so that others can respond proactively to those differences. At its best, labeling surrounds children with well-funded advocates and identifies concerns to which caring adults can respond.

However, many of us use labels unwisely. We give them too much authority. We begin innocently enough, labeling children in order to flag a concern. Then, maybe because of ignorance or hopelessness, we slide into believing and acting upon those labels as prophetic and immutable. When we don't limit labels to being only a first step in recognizing potential concerns and in caring for children, when we don't balance those identifiers with the hope of an At-Promise perspective, those labels can lead us in the wrong direction.

We Respond in Fear

Maybe you are worrying about the character shortcomings in your advantaged child for the first time. Maybe concern over your child's deficits is making you shiver. Whenever we run up against the threats our children walk with daily, each of us must choose how to respond. Sadly, we often choose to fear, though we may not recognize it as such. We'll learn to identify hidden fear later, but for now let's recognize that one way we give in to fear is to believe and surrender to the predictions of negative labels.

When we believe that risks have overtaken our children, we are afraid to hope deeply for their futures. Research tells us that parents often have less hope for their children's future than their children do![7] We anticipate their likely failures and may be inclined to abandon them to defeat. By embracing negative implications of labels, we tell our children that they are inclined to fail. We begin to act against our deepest desires for their success by guarding and lowering our expectations of them. We fixate on the deficits in them that we want to eliminate. We fear for them, and they learn to believe that fear.

With at-risk eyesight, we expect to see children fall into dangerous crevasses. Then at-risk thinking tells us to toss ropes of support and encouragement to those tumbling kids. Unfortunately, experts tell us, their problems go so deep that our ropes may be too short to reach them or may be too frayed to pull them out.

This approach contradicts what my father taught me [Tim] about driving at night. He told me not to stare at the headlights coming in the opposite direction. If I did, he said, instead of looking away from them and in the direction I was traveling, I would head right toward them. The lights' intensity would blind me; I would stray into the wrong lane; and I would crash.

Negative labels are like those oncoming headlights. They are sharing our road and are part of our experience, as is any adversity. We are driving past them, carrying kids we care about. Though those labels illuminate our children's condition, they can also blind us and lead us astray if we stare at them.

As a young student teacher in a high school outside of Chicago, I [Tim] saw exactly how this works. The school was notorious for the activities of three distinct gangs. Security guards patrolled the halls; we contended with fights, poverty, and fear every day. The neighborhood was so dangerous that I had a difficult time finding a college professor willing to supervise my student-teaching experience. (The professor who finally agreed to brave the school's parking lot, Marilyn Scribner, had just written a book on self-defense!)

Kids in our school were fearful and underachieving; I could see why. When survival is a child's top priority, learning rarely fits into the equation. That semester I crossed ten names off my student rosters—names of students jailed, injured in gang-related conflicts, or killed. I was devastated.

Experienced teachers, my mentors, did not want my self-confidence rattled by the behavior of my at-risk students. So these veterans quickly prescribed a remedy. They told me that I couldn't have helped those kids anyway. They said I needed to remind myself that these were at-risk kids. I should just be glad that I only lost ten and that all the others showed up for class!

When we think this way, and children around us fail, at-risk thinking says, *Who expected anything different?* Students like those in Chicago resemble the third-class passengers on the Titanic, who had no access to lifeboats. In life's war they are the casualties whom society factors in as collateral damage before the battle begins. Defined as at-risk kids, they fulfill the anticipated-failure quota in our schools.

The complex needs of children give some of us a terrifying sense of inadequacy. We do not know what to do, and that scares us. But when we attempt to solve problems with fear-based at-risk labeling, we can ultimately do more harm than good. The truth is that when we treat labeled children as if risk has already conquered them, those labels rob kids of hope for themselves and rob us of hope for them, putting them in a position of even greater peril. Without hope, we don't trust very much or try very hard.

We Can Respond with Hope

In light of very real risks, we do have choices to make. We can choose to live in a state of denial about the barrage of challenges kids encounter. We can slap convenient labels on children to justify their failures and shortcomings. We can let fear cloud our thinking and our actions.

Or we can learn about and develop an At-Promise perspective. So before we proceed, we'd like you to look at Table 2.1, which outlines the premises underlying the At-Promise paradigm and contrasts them with at-risk and advantaged thinking.

Table 2.1. At-Promise Paradigm Shift.

At-Risk and Advantaged Paradigms	At-Promise Paradigm
Motivated by fear	Motivated by love
Define *success* as having more education, money, power, achievement, and influence	Defines *success* as contributing positively to the moral and social fabric of society
View children in light of what they have and don't have: assets and deficits	Views children in light of who they are: created in God's likeness
Contribute to children's success by adults' offering them provisions or programs that protect them from adversity	Contributes to children's success by adults' cultivating and modeling their own positive character as they build trusting relationships with children; recognizes that adversity is necessary to that process
Emphasize protecting children from failure and salvaging lives damaged by adversity	Emphasizes using adversity to construct character and facilitate success in young people

Illustrating the At-Promise Paradigm Shift

Author Anne Lamott encourages other writers to cast light on life's confusing, painful circumstances, to put life's dark places into words. She writes: "The light [we] shine on this hole, this pit, helps us cut away or step around the brush and brambles; then we can dance around the rim of the abyss, holler into it, measure it, throw rocks in it, and still not fall in. It can no longer swallow us up. And we can get on with things."[8]

Can't her words also apply to us and our children? When we practice At-Promise thinking, we can affirm the children we care about and help them interpret their dim cavern of difficulties. We can illuminate it and walk them through it. Then this dark cave can become a place of triumph for children and the adults who treasure them. Admitting risk and staring our fears in the face can lead to this kind of victory dance in our families. So let's get on with things. Grab a flashlight and a few rocks, and come along.

Remember . . .

- When we line up all the threats to children, we can identify fully 100 percent of all kids as at risk for failure.
- When we pretend that advantages alone empower kids to succeed, we are in denial.
- Like tattoos, labels mark young people. They don't wash off, and they are constant reminders of how we perceive them.
- The truth is that when we treat labeled children as if risk has already conquered them, those labels rob kids of hope for themselves and rob us of hope for them, putting them in a position of even greater peril.

Chapter Three

Fear: Love's Counterfeit

Love takes off masks that we fear we cannot live
without and know we cannot live within.

—*James Baldwin*

I [Tim] pride myself on being able to maintain an air of composure in stressful situations. When challenges cross my path, I keep my cool—with one exception. I am deathly afraid of snakes. Don't ask me why; I don't know. But when I see a snake of any size, my heart pounds and my skin goes pale. I lose all composure. No, that's putting it too mildly. What really happens is that I panic and just want to escape. In fact, I am sure that a group of German tourists still talks about the lunatic in Turkey who ran screaming and flailing into the Mediterranean surf when his laughing wife flung a dead snake at him.

To my chagrin my kids remind me of that story every chance they get. But no amount of teasing changes my reaction. The moment I encounter a snake, the only thing I can think about is how to save myself. Fear overpowers all rational thought. Not a pretty picture.

What Do We Fear?

The fears we have about our children failing are a little bit like my fear of snakes. When it comes to kids you care about, what are your deepest fears? Take some time to write those fears down, so you can see them in black and white.

1. _____

2. _____

3. _____

Did you fill in the list? Good. We'll come back to it at the end of the chapter.

Fear's Impact

It's pretty safe to assume that anyone reading this book cares about children. Those of us who have embraced at-risk and advantaged thinking love our children as much as those of us who have adopted the At-Promise paradigm. And yet the illustration of the At-Promise paradigm shift at the end of Chapter Two describes fear as a key player behind the at-risk and advantaged paradigms. How is that true? Unless we learn to spot the many ways that fear can influence us, we won't be able to tell when our care for children is compromised by fear. That's why we're dedicating a chapter to explaining just how fear can masquerade as love.

For most of my [Cheryl's] first three decades of life, I had little understanding of the role fear played in my family—and in me. My fear wasn't driven by isolated events or objects, like Tim's feared snakes. Instead, fear acted like an offshore undertow, hauling me in a current that could have drowned me and perpetuating a pattern that had coursed through generations of my family. On the following pages, I'd like to tell you that story. Sometimes we can best see how fear's layers influence families by watching it travel through the years.

Fear does that, you know. It can drive a life without ever being identified. Fear can mutate, prevent, or restrict our intimacies, choices of spouses, educational decisions, careers, parenting styles, hobbies, health, personalities, life expectancies—pretty much everything—all with a current we fail to recognize because it flows beneath the surface. We often fail to recognize fear because it disguises itself so well.

And fear doesn't stop with you and me. We can also transmit fear from generation to generation. In doing so we can sabotage our most caring efforts to grow children At Promise. Have you ever stood between two mirrors, positioned so that they bounce reflections back and forth at each other, on to infinity? Our perceptions can ricochet like that, reverberating back and forth between us and the kids we care about. Here's how: a child acts. The parent, watching, reflects an interpretation of that behavior back to the child, who processes that interpretation, believes it, and bounces back another image conforming to the parent's reflection. Again the mirroring parent picks up the picture and sends it back to the child. Those exchanges continue down through the years. The young person, seeing the image so many times, solidifies that fleeting, transient image into fact.

Unlike disinterested mirrors, we can choose what we reflect to the young people we care about. What we choose depends upon what we believe. And what we believe will have either love or fear at its core. Therefore, spotting fear is a vital step in ditching at-risk thinking and in cultivating promise character that will enable us, by God's power, to lead children into the process of success.

Family Lines

At age twelve, my [Cheryl's] grandfather lost his dad, a trapper and fisherman, in the territory we now call Alaska. Eyes fell on young Syd, the family's eldest boy, to support his mother and three siblings. So he quit school and got a job. Several jobs, actually. Ensuing years found him working in remote logging operations as a "whistle punk" for the primitive "steam donkey" that helped yard logs out of the woods. He also crewed for fish buyers in southeastern Alaska and spiked boom logs at lumber mills. He worked hard and—I believe—afraid, though he buried it beneath layers of self-sufficiency and toughness. He was just a boy, but his family depended on his earnings to buy groceries and pay bills. Work and workers in the pioneer Northwest were dangerous and rough. Logs, sea, and weapons saved and took lives.

Through it all Gramps learned two principles that he followed into his old age. First, he learned that the harder he worked, the more money he could make. Second, he believed that money would protect the women in his care from destitution. His younger brother would eventually earn a wage, but his mother and sisters needed him. He had seen how poor widows took in boarders or how they barely eked out a living on seamstress and laundress wages. He had watched them die young from exhaustion. As long as he had an ounce of breath left, his mother, Mary Emma, and sisters, Irene and Virginia, would never suffer like that. And so Syd worked night and day, living by industry and wits.

Shortly after the Great Depression burrowed into the 1930s, Gramps married Imogene, my peaceable grandmother, who fit well under his protective wing or, if she didn't stay out of the way, would be toppled by the energy in it. She deferred to his dynamic style, content to let him take charge and take care of her.

Catastrophes just urged Gramps on. By the time their only child, my mother, was born, fire had charred their home. Later a gasoline explosion laid up Gramps for a while. Nonetheless, he had a new family to care for. And his goal had broadened. Now he did not want to protect his mother, wife, and daughter only from the financial destitution he had feared in childhood but from any adversity. He believed that the money that came from his tireless efforts could buy them shelter from all pain.

He loved his wife and daughter deeply and showed it, he believed, by pouring himself into new businesses, diversifying and succeeding in financial undertakings. With relentless drive and enthusiasm, he tackled new projects and fed his bank account, which grew even in the Depression. He brought home not just the bacon but the whole sow—and created a world of comfort for the women in his life. With whatever fortitude necessary, he would intercept and eradicate all discomfort.

He tried to meet not only their physical needs but their complicated emotional ones—with money. Not because he was selfish but because down deep he was afraid, and he had never learned a better way. He needed simple solutions in a frightening world and felt out of control without them. When his wife asked if they could see more of him, spend time with him, he felt accused and worked all the harder.

World War II, with its accompanying uncertainty, casualties, rations, and blackouts, only drove him deeper into his fear pattern. He worked nonstop. Somehow, though Hitler was advancing and nations were falling, he would create a haven for his women, guard them from danger.

He did, physically. They lived in a beautiful home and after the war drove Cadillacs and Lincolns. Gram wore furs and jewelry they purchased on their extended travels. His daughter had the best of everything: lessons, clothes, private schooling, community prestige. The best of everything . . .

Except her dad. She learned early that he was unavailable emotionally. He wanted to hear nothing about any problems she might have with friends or relationships. Not because he didn't care but because he cared so much. When she hurt, he hurt, and he couldn't patch emotional pain with a dollar. In order to feel like he was caring for his family, he needed to feel like he was in control, and unhappy feelings made him feel powerless, as if he had failed the family. So he denied any relational problems and wouldn't discuss them. In reply his wife and daughter learned to shove feelings underground and didn't talk about them either.

Mother and daughter were very different. Syd's wife, my grandmother, was mild and tractable and avoided conflict whenever possible. Just as she deferred to her husband, she acquiesced to her strong-willed daughter. Long before adolescence my mom learned that although she couldn't deeply connect with her father, neither did she have to submit to his authority. He wouldn't discipline her. It was simply too painful for him. Even so, he wanted her to be a perfect child. When she wasn't, he believed he had somehow failed her. Their quarrels widened the gap. Both felt incapable of pleasing the other. Without her husband's backing, Gram had little success correcting her feisty, often unhappy daughter—and attempted to placate her instead.

The result of these dynamics? After Gramps lost his father, he swore that his family would never know such pain. In protecting them he did not equip his daughter for life's inevitable trials. Nor did he understand that he had passed his inner ache on to her. As it often does, unacknowledged fear perpetuates the pain it seeks to avoid. Gramps' fear, born at the loss of his father, drove him and betrayed him; it kept him from truly caring for his daughter. Ironically, in many ways she didn't have a dad either.

Then, when my mother was seventeen, a classmate captured her attention and ardor. Handsome, talented, intelligent, Bill plotted an ambitious future and wanted to include her. His edginess enticed her—but repelled her parents. Where she experienced his charm, affection, and approval, Gram and Gramps saw his instability and questionable integrity. Furthermore, his parents had lost their farm, sold their mules, and left the swirling dust of Oklahoma more than a dozen years before, scrapping their way out Route 66 to California, where they followed the crops north. No one from that kind of upheaval and poverty, my grandparents believed, could possibly care for their precious only child.

Their protests flopped like just-caught trout on dry ground. Whether her parents liked it or not, she would marry Bill as soon as they graduated from high school. She would wring out all that childhood loneliness and distance and soak her life in a new family that would give her what she believed her first one never did. Despite their disapproval and true to their pattern, my grandparents gave her a lavish wedding. I was conceived that night.

Within the next five years, my parents had four children. My mother was desperately unhappy—and afraid. Having been shielded from trials rather than trained for them, she was oarless and adrift with a pack of kids in a sea of adversity she didn't understand. My father hauled us from state to state and job to job, his eye always on the next deal and the greener opportunity in the next town. We four children slept in one double bed (which one of us usually wet) in a trail of rental houses with empty kitchen cupboards. We were weaned on insecurity and anger. Our daddy rarely came home when we were awake, and when he did, he and Mom fought. Before I turned six, they divorced, in an era when few couples split up. Our grandparents took us all in, and my mother went to work in Gramps's business. We rarely saw my dad after that. Fear had done its dirty work. A new generation of children was fatherless.

Fear makes people selfish, and I am no exception. My early lessons—that tomorrow we may have no food or no home or no daddy—made me fiercely self-protective. Only years later, as I began to let God love me, did I learn to recognize fear's disguises and its many manifestations in my life. I also realized that the fear current flowing through generations of my family was not unique. Fear's ancient pattern—introduced in Genesis 3, when the serpent tempted Eve—shows up in me, as it shows up in every single person to one degree or another, because we are sinful people, distanced at birth from the love and care of our Father God. What could be more frightening?

Fear's Distinguishing Traits

Just as Tim's fear of snakes overpowers his loving, rational behavior, fear like mine or yours can also distract us from the At-Promise identity of children we care about. Four distinct behaviors result from that fear. See if you recognize them.

Control

First, fear makes us want to control things. We want to orchestrate others and our environment to keep ourselves—and loved ones—safe. We become less flexible, more rigid in our attempts to create and preserve a predictable environment. Eve didn't want to leave knowledge in God's hands and trust His control. She wanted that knowledge and control herself. Gramps wanted to control his family's emotional and physical environment in order to protect them from pain. My mother chose to marry someone she would try unsuccessfully to control.

When our children were born, I wanted to control their experiences so that they would never have to experience the family pain I did not yet understand. Like Gramps, I loved my offspring and wanted them to do well, but I also feared that their failures would mean I had fallen short in caring for them. I thought I was responsible for more than faithful parenting and believed that the outcome of my parenting was up to me. Though I had chosen to trust God, an unsurrendered part of me still wanted to break our family's pattern in my own strength instead of His. I had yet to learn that if anything would perpetuate an undesirable pattern, my own fearfulness would!

Control issues take many forms. A caring educator or youth worker may give up on a child because she has so little control over the child's circumstances—and fears they are too difficult to surmount. Or a caring adult may fear that she will be the only one significantly involved in the child's life, fear that she may be unable to control the demands on her time, and fear burnout.

Denial

Second, fear makes us deny frightening realities about ourselves and our world. We look at ourselves less honestly. Just as Adam and Eve hid from God and blamed others for their actions, so too do we hide emotionally and blame others. We deny the truth. My grandfather denied the fact that his wife and daughter were hurting and that his money could not lessen their pain. My mother blamed her father, my father, and the demands of us children for her anger and lack of peace. I too wanted to blame circumstances or people when I was fearful and overprotective, rather than to see how my chosen responses contributed to my anxiety. I was dishonest with myself.

When we are attempting to build relationship with young people, our denial and glossing over our own struggles with shortcomings, sin, or trials may deprive those kids of useful knowledge about adversity. When we pretend that we have it all together and don't struggle with anything, we do children a serious disservice and can drive them further underground into more dishonesty.

Isolation

Third, fear isolates us. Fear of judgment, exposure, domination, intimacy, or other threats prompts us to wall people out either physically, spiritually, or emotionally. If we do hook up with others, we may choose to spend time with those who are as afraid as we are. That way no one will try to draw closer than is comfortable for either. We will mimic one another's denial, avoid intimacy, and dodge conversation that could leave us vulnerable to rejection or condemnation—or that will shatter our image. My grandfather avoided the challenges of intimacy by burying himself in his work. My mother married an unfaithful man running from his own past and with whom a trusting relationship was impossible. For years I avoided deep friendships, afraid to trust anyone with my most vulnerable feelings.

Youth workers may spend many hours with children but through no fault of the child's may be too afraid to build genuine trust, too cautious to draw close enough to extend a lifeline that can lead the kids through youth's blizzard of struggles. Prompted by tragic stories of abuse by caregivers, teachers, and clergy, well-meaning folks attempting to keep appropriate boundaries with kids may sabotage opportunities for trust by staying emotionally distant from children. They may construct a superficial connection that parodies true relationship.

Hopelessness

Finally, fear robs us of hope. When problems land on us, if we're afraid, we have a much harder time believing that we have God's power available to us to handle them. We lack a grounded optimism and may instead expect defeat. Gramps was afraid that Mom could not learn to handle affliction, so he tried to keep it away from her. He had no hope in her ability to grow strong because of it. Mom's fear fixed her focus on the worst in us kids, which she projected into our futures. When we looked in her mirroring eyes, we did not see hope. When our young son pushed his sister's tricycle under my car tires, I too made fear-based predictions. Adults, seeing kids as at risk, can lose hope that those children will ever be able to leap the crevasses threatening to swallow them.

Fear really does subvert our best intentions for our children. Like a boil deep beneath the skin, fear can poison healthy interactions. If it's severe enough, it can taint the relational bloodstream and contaminate everyone in its path. No wonder God inspired the words "Do not be afraid," which appear over ninety times in the Bible, not to mention hundreds of other instructions about fear. It's deadly and occupies space in our minds and hearts that we could instead fill with love.

Facing Our Fears

Look back to the beginning of this chapter—at your list of fears for children. What are you doing with those alarming fears? Entertaining them? Believing them? Giving in to them? Overreacting to them? Do you respond to them with controlling behavior, denial and blame, isolation, or hopelessness?

Sometimes when we face the scary realities of our children's risks, our thoughts are about saving ourselves. As Tim's reaction to the flung snake displayed, fear often leads to self-preservation. Are your fears concerned with your own reputation? Your status as a family? Your dreams for your kids? Your fear of failure? Your fear of pain? I know that some of my fears have been.

Love Drives Out Fear

When we love with our own intellect, emotions, or human strength, we will not succeed fully. Because we are imperfect human beings, fear and the selfishness it feeds will still lurk deep in our motives. Consequently, we will love imperfectly. All we have to do is look at our relationships to know how true that is!

But God's "perfect love drives out fear" (1 John 4:18). Instead of responding to children with fear camouflaged as love, we can learn how real love works. This concept started to make sense to me when I realized that God hadn't been distant from me; I had been distant from Him because I was afraid to trust Him! Once I decided to look for, acknowledge, and respond to his love for me, I became less afraid. My attitudes and behaviors began to change. Exchanging fear for love has had distinct manifestations in my life, and it characterizes At-Promise living. Here's what happens.

Flexibility

First, when we let love drive out our fear, we gradually decrease our controlling behavior. We realize that we are not fatherless; God is the daddy who loves us and will act in our very best interests if we will just trust Him. He has a plan for all those circumstances and people we are trying to manipulate. When we are not expending so much energy trying to control everyone and everything else, we can be more in control of ourselves and will ultimately have far greater impact. We can be more flexible and more influential by example.

Don't be surprised if you notice your fears exploding as you initially release control. Surrender itself can be a scary process. Though your control has artificially subdued your fears over time, they aren't gone. You can only truly dismantle them through surrender.

Honesty

Second, love allows us to be honest—and courageous. We don't have to deny and blame anymore. We don't need to hide from each other. We no longer need to run and protect ourselves at others' expense. No matter how badly we have messed up with our kids, we can come to God and find a fresh start. He doesn't condemn us. He loves us so completely that we can be honest with Him and with ourselves and still feel safe. What a relief!

That safety enables us to be honest with those we love too. We can acknowledge our own mistakes to them. We can apologize. We can talk directly about difficult issues without feeling threatened. We can teach and discipline children lovingly—not because we are perfect models but because He loves, forgives, and empowers us. Though I still consider myself a beginner, learning this kind of honesty and vulnerability has improved and deepened my relationships and has helped my kids to develop their own willingness to grow.

Connection

Third, love connects us. Where fear once isolated us, the safe, pure love that comes from God allows us to develop deep, trusting relationships with friends, spouses, relatives, and children we care about. When I was living more fearfully, I thought I understood intimacy, but I really had no idea what it meant. Genuine connection scared me. Sometimes it still does, but I am learning to experience true emotional and spiritual intimacy. I'm realizing what so many have learned before me—that as our trust grows, we are drawn to and we seek out like-minded and like-hearted people and experience that intimacy with them. We become emotionally, spiritually, and physically trustworthy. We no longer feel alone, mistrustful, and on our own. We can relax and enjoy life with the young people in our care, and we can join together with them to serve others.

Hope

Finally, love gives us hope. No matter how grim a report our eyes and ears may give us about our kids, we believe God, who tells us that He is "able to do immeasurably more than all we ask or imagine, according to his power that is at work within us" (Ephesians 3:20). When I imagine kids' futures, I don't "awful-ize" as I once would have, at least not for very long. Instead, I stake my life—and the lives of the children I care about—on the fact that "nothing is impossible with God" (Luke 1:37). This certainty gives me—as it can give us all—the courage to lead our risk-facing, At-Promise kids through adversity and into the success God has planned for them.

How do we know all this? Because God's love is driving out fear in our [Tim's and Cheryl's] own lives daily. He can do the same in yours too. As He does, He will empower you to build promise character into both yourself and the children you care about.

Remember . . .

- Fear really does subvert our best intentions for our children. Like a boil deep beneath the skin, fear can poison healthy interactions.
- Sometimes when we face the scary realities of our children's risks, our thoughts are about saving ourselves.
- When we are not expending so much energy trying to control everyone and everything else, we can be more in control of ourselves and will ultimately have far greater impact.

Part Two

Requirements for Growth

At-Promise Principles 1 and 2

Chapter Four

Adversity and Pain
Can Lead to Growth

Adversity draws men together and produces beauty
and harmony in life's relationships, just as the cold
of winter produces ice-flowers on the window
panes, which vanish with the warmth.

—*Søren Kierkegaard*

I [Tim] was born in Dallas, Texas, but moved to France, the land of baguettes, brie, and escargot, when I was four years old. (Somehow, the thought of eating snails appealed to me a lot more at that age than it does now.) I attended school in the French system until the eighth grade. Much to my mother's dismay, I quickly abandoned English in favor of the most popular language on the neighborhood soccer field. French served me well until my family and I moved back to the United States. Despite my knack for languages, I arrived in Havertown, Pennsylvania, at the age of thirteen with abysmal English reading and writing skills.

Anxious to classify my needs so that they could give me the most appropriate support, my new U.S. school tested my abilities. In their zeal they gave me an IQ test—in English, of course. The school psychologist analyzed the results, which declared me to be "educable mentally retarded." (This was all my sisters needed to confirm their lifelong suspicions about my mental capacity!) The diagnosis qualified me for special education classes. I, along with a variety of special-needs students, spent the majority of my eighth-grade year in a special education resource center.

The "mentally retarded" label hung on me more heavily than the name tag I was required to wear around my neck in case I got lost. The school saw me as at risk, and indeed they were right. I felt stupid. I secretly feared that the IQ results and the school counselor's verdict sentenced me to a life of dumbness. Even without a bad day at the testing center, it does not take much to shake a thirteen-year-old's self-confidence. I was confused and scared about what this might mean for the rest of my life.

Most parents would have removed their child from the school in order to protect him from this kind of negative experience, but not mine. Although they never once doubted my abilities, and rejected any label the school was trying to place on me, they also saw the positive effects this experience would have on me for the rest of my life. First of all, they knew that the individualized attention I was getting in that small-group setting was exactly what I needed to catch up in English. Second, they wanted me to experience firsthand that what people said or thought about me was not necessarily the truth.

From that point on (as my wife has come to find out), no one could ever convince me that I couldn't do something. When my tenth-grade English teacher told me that I did not have what it took to go to college, I refused to believe him. In fact, I told him that he was wrong to his face—which he was!

My parents also knew that going through this adverse situation with their help would strengthen my relationship with them. Through it all they believed in me. They saw my promise when no one else would.

AT-PROMISE PRINCIPLE 1: Adversity provides a catalyst for a child's character growth and is essential to success.

We easily struggle over this principle. Some people can misinterpret and misuse it, using the concept to try to justify their abuse or neglect of the children in their care. But most of us simply do not want pain. As we said before, adversity scares us, and rightfully so, particularly when it affects our children. We have trouble trusting that pain can be good for our kids. We are wise to be cautious. Without a caring, trusted adult to guide kids, adversity, pain, and trials can devastate or destroy them.

When an adult comes alongside a child and helps him interpret what's happening, those trials become catalysts for growth and ultimate success. In fact, pain is absolutely essential to building successful individuals.

We are not alone in suggesting that adversity contributes to a child's success. Dr. Sybil Wolin sees that adversity is a necessary component to developing resiliency, which we'll discuss in Chapter Six. In her book *The Struggle to be Strong,* Dr. Wolin looks at young people who have overcome or are in the process of overcoming adversity in their lives. She suggests that a child's resiliency develops through "the process of struggling with hardship. That process progresses by accumulating small successes that occur side by side with failures, setbacks, and disappointments."[1]

Dr. Michael Rutter, professor of developmental psychopathology, says that a child's immune system is not developed by being protected from infection but rather by the body's struggle to overcome infection. Likewise, he suggests that although science has limited "systematic evidence" of this, it makes sense to believe that this principle of immunization would also apply to a child's social development.[2] Maybe the struggles inherent in getting along with others are essential to developing strong social health.

Traditionally, resiliency research identifies "protective factors" that allow children to overcome adversity.[3] These characteristics in children allow them to beat the odds and succeed in spite of adversity. The At-Promise perspective goes one step further, suggesting that adversity, in the context of a caring adult relationship, may in fact contribute to a child's success. We recognize that resiliency cannot develop in the absence of trials and adversity; consequently, trials are not the enemy of success. They can in fact contribute to it.

The idea that trials and adversity contribute positively to an individual's strength of character, including one's perseverance, is a long-standing religious belief. "Consider it pure joy," the Bible tells us, "when you face trials of many kinds, because you know that the testing of your faith develops perseverance" (James 1:2–3). Beyond Judeo-Christian beliefs, we regularly read or hear stories of individuals who have benefited from adverse situations in their lives.[4]

Even terrible forms of adversity—such as being tortured or imprisoned for one's beliefs—can deepen resolve, conviction, and fearlessness in entire communities. I [Tim] had an opportunity to speak with Ambassador John Hanford about the effects of religious persecution. Ambassador Hanford is the U.S. ambassador at large for religious freedom and the senior advisor to Secretary Powell and President Bush on matters concerning religious freedom around the world. He spoke with conviction and compassion when he said: "Americans believe that no human right is more important than our ability to seek and to know God. This right was foundational in the establishment of our country and one that needs to be defended." He went on to say: "Persecution does not work. When governments persecute people for their faith, it only strengthens their conviction and resolve. Even in the face of mistreatment and death, people become fearless and willing to sacrifice their lives for their beliefs."

Although no one is advocating religious persecution and we all believe we must do everything in our power to stop persecution around the world, we are convinced that persecution, like any adversity, can and does build strength. Cultures and individuals throughout history have demonstrated this fact.

Three key points about adversity and its accompanying pain have emerged from our research and experience as educators, parents, and members of families and communities:

- Children who have not experienced adversity are at risk of not reaching their full potential.
- Children who grow up in adverse circumstances without a significant relationship with a caring, trusted adult may be overwhelmed by their trials.
- Adversity, in the context of a relationship with a trusted adult, is critical to a child's success in life.

The Absence of Adversity Creates Risk

Every sports enthusiast knows that our bodies need resistance in order to develop strength. However, we often forget that the absence of resistance causes our muscles to atrophy. In the same way, children must experience resistance in order to grow. When we remove opportunities for them to struggle, we restrict the full development of their innate promise.

Luke Thomas (a pseudonym) is a businessman who contributes positively to our society by overseeing several philanthropic organizations that help young people. He shared with me [Tim] that his mother, a caring and brilliant woman, did everything in her power to protect him from the challenges of life. She wanted to offer him success on a platter, but in his view, this "indulged" childhood became the most noticeable risk factor in his life and the one thing that could have stood in the way of his eventual success. He said, "The world at large is not prepared to spoil you, and if you get to be fourteen or fifteen and you have the notion that the world is there for your benefit, well, there is a lot of risk for a kid like that." He explained that an untested childhood leaves young people shocked and deeply disappointed once they become "buried in the realities of life." In his view the effect of this unexpected adversity can derail indulged children, whose lack of preparation for struggle can be a serious barrier to success. In his teens he realized that "the world was not as easy a place as my mother made it for me."

The book of Genesis in the Bible tells the story of Joseph, the indulged favorite son of his father, Jacob. Not only did his father love him more than his other brothers, but Jacob also gave him a colorful, incredibly crafted robe that shouted of Joseph's favored status.

Oblivious to the effects his pampered treatment had on his brothers, Joseph actually wore the robe in their presence. Then he flaunted his superiority by describing a dream in which all his brothers bowed down to him. Clearly, deferential treatment in Joseph's privileged childhood had put him at severe risk of mistreatment by his jealous brothers.

Like young Joseph, indulged, overprotected children are less likely to have developed the character traits necessary to their success. Because they lack the schooling that adversity gives, their promise remains latent, inactive, undeveloped.

Adversity Initiates Reality Checks

Research indicates that children who "face particularly difficult experiences" encounter "reality checks." These experiences encourage kids to develop positive goals.[5] In the landmark study found in the book *Cradles of Eminence,* Victor and Mildred Goertzel explored the home backgrounds of three hundred highly successful people, including Helen Keller, Franklin D. Roosevelt, Winston Churchill, and Albert Einstein. Detailed investigation of their early lives revealed facts that affirm the value that adversity can have. Consider these facts:

- Three-fourths of the individuals they surveyed were raised either in poverty; in broken homes; or by rejecting, overpossessive, or controlling parents.
- Seventy-four of eighty-five writers of fiction or drama, and sixteen of twenty poets, came from homes where families played out tense psychological dramas.
- Physical handicaps such as blindness, deafness, or crippled limbs characterized over one-fourth of the sample.[6]

Joseph's reality checks came when his jealous, spiteful brothers sold him into slavery and he ended up in prison. The wisdom that came from those God-guided trials eventually set him at the top of Egyptian government.

Like Joseph's, reality checks can be dramatic: dropping out of school, becoming pregnant, or undergoing drug rehabilitation. They can also consist of other less hair-raising experiences: being cut from the basketball team, getting poor grades, ending a romance, or losing a school election.

But whatever the trials, if our children experience them in the context of a caring, trusted relationship, those trials are more likely to lead to growth, rebalance, self-reflection, and ultimately victory.

Golfer Tiger Woods's dad understood that principle and used it to train Tiger in mental toughness. As Earl Woods put it in his book, *Training a Tiger,* "Tiger and I have a very strong personal relationship based upon mutual trust and respect. That is the only way I would have considered putting him through this kind of training." That training consisted of Earl dropping clubs just as his son took his swing, crowing when he putted, tossing a ball across his line of vision, and doing his level best to distract Tiger in whatever way he could. Earl said that he exposed Tiger to every "insidious trick that any future opponent could pull on him. . . . He later told me it was the most difficult experience of his entire life. At times he was so angry with me he wanted to destroy his clubs. . . . He certainly wouldn't have wished this training on any other human being. But he learned. And he became mentally tough." Earl later told his son that he would never meet anyone tougher.[7]

Tiger Woods, as we all know, continues to win tournaments.

Adversity Leads to Self-Reflection

Losing is never easy, particularly when our children lose at something they have strived hard to achieve. With failures come painful feelings of inadequacy, inferiority, abandonment, and—if appropriate—conviction of one's wrongdoing. Without clear guidance, these feelings can send a child on a downward spiral to despair.

On the other hand, trusted adults can help children turn failure into a positive experience by encouraging the self-analysis that can happen because of failure. Educational research shows that self-reflection, sometimes called metacognition, is a critical and essential contributor to the learning process.[8] Self-reflection is the most important ingredient for learning from our mistakes, but it does not often happen in a relational vacuum. Caring adults are key contributors to the learning process because of their ability to listen empathically and then offer perspective and hope when children are experiencing failure. Sometimes being able to say, "Been there, learned from that!" can help kids look at some of their challenges from a new perspective.

Luke Thomas, whom we mentioned earlier, told another story that illustrates how the self-reflective process can lead us from failure to victory. During his senior year in high school, he ran for student body president. As he tells it, "I was beaten pretty badly. That was a grave disappointment and generated a lot of self-reflection. I began to think about why so many people voted for the other guy . . . about things that distinguished him from me. Those were very worthwhile observations." He went on from there to modify his own character.

Adversity Fosters Growth

Jeff Jani, a former Microsoft executive and entrepreneur, talked to me [Tim] about what it was like growing up in the home of a high-achieving, prosperous father. Jeff's dad was one of Disney's top executives, and as a result, Jeff grew up in a home with all the benefits that came along with money. As a boy he traveled around the world, received a first-rate education, and met and interacted with powerful individuals. Nevertheless, he concluded that the largest struggle he faced was growing up in his father's shadow. It was difficult for the young Jeff to understand the lines between what dreams belonged to his father and what dreams belonged to him.

But when Jeff was twenty-three, his father contracted Lou Gehrig's disease; he died three years later. Clearly, the adversity Jeff experienced during his father's illness and death became a catalyst for his enormous success. Listen carefully to the words of a man who experienced the deepest kind of adversity, the loss of a loved one.

> I would say that the tragedy . . . forced me to examine a lot [of my own identity issues] and gave me huge obstacles to overcome. What

did this mean for me? How would I carry on the business without my dad? Where was I going to go with my life? If my family fell apart, did that mean I would fall apart? Who was I going to be?

No one would wish this kind of adversity on any young person. However, trials and adversity of this magnitude happen every day. The question is this: Are we willing to turn these events into training grounds for growth? Jeff looks back at overcoming his struggles as foundational in discovering his own identity, developing his faith in God, and preparing him for future challenges. "That was a big breakthrough, coming out of all that pain. Huge, accelerating personal growth came out of this total chaos and destruction. It allowed me the opportunity to grow, which gave me the foundation to be who I am today. The influence and success that I've been able to have is because I was able to figure that out."

Why We Overprotect Children

So pain can be useful. Easy for you to say, you may be thinking. *Adversity may very well have its benefits, but I still think kids are better off without it. I don't like to hurt, and I certainly don't like to see children I love suffer either. Besides, don't I have the responsibility to keep my children safe? To protect them harmful circumstances?*

When we protect our children from hurt too much, they may develop a distorted sense of self, thinking that they are either more resilient than they are or less capable than they are. God demonstrates this in trees. A tree may grow tall and look strong, but unless it has been in the wind, it's likely to blow over in a storm. Wind, you see, helps strengthen a tree by building sturdiness in the trunk and encouraging root growth. Although a sheltered tree can tolerate only small gusts, a tree that has grown up with wind can withstand terrible storms. So it is with children. Protecting them from failure may boost their self-esteem temporarily but in the end may weaken their emotional immune system because of the absence of valuable adversity and hurt in their lives.

Similarly, when we refuse to find the usefulness in harm that even the wisest among us would never have chosen, we keep children victimized with hopelessness and helplessness. We deny them the redeeming power of tragedy transformed, of life coming from death. As strange as it may seem, such resurrections happen every day.

While there is no doubt that parents and teachers are responsible for protecting children from destructive levels of adversity, we have seen that a certain degree of adversity is necessary for a child's growth. So why do we insulate kids from useful trials? Let's take a look at some of the reasons.

We Overprotect Because We Overvalue Self-Esteem

Americans have had a long-standing romance with an imaginary friend: self-esteem. Heralded as the savior capable of fixing today's educational system, crime rates, and economic recession, the feel-good-about-yourself message finds its way to the top of most educational priority lists. Very little research, however, suggests that positive self-esteem induces good performance in school and in life.[9] In fact, studies show that individuals who commit violent crimes have inappropriately high self-esteem![10]

Because we have erroneously established self-esteem as the ticket to our children's success, we guard our children against anything that makes them feel bad about themselves. Our thought process works like this:

1. If my child faces trials, she will at some point experience failure.
2. If she fails, she will feel badly about herself.
3. If she feels badly about herself, she will develop negative self-esteem.
4. If she has low self-esteem, she cannot be successful in life.
5. Therefore, I cannot afford to let my child experience trials and adversity.

Politicians convincingly deliver the self-esteem message. School districts have jumped on board the self-esteem bandwagon. Errantly, both regularly isolate the concept from either an unconditional, God-given identity or from self-efficacy resulting from accomplishment. The problem? Positive self-esteem apart from divine identity or achievement will not help children become successful. And when we try to guard their self-esteem from realistic challenges, we can end up overprotecting them.

We Overprotect Because We Lack Confidence

Some of us protect children from adversity because we are afraid of their incompetence. Before you disagree, ask yourself this: Don't many of us fear that children cannot stand up to the hardship of keeping a bedroom clean every day, handling chores around the house, attending play practice, and completing homework? We fear that our children cannot stand up to hardship, so we let them off or do the work for them. When they run out of money, we slip them a bill so that they have some spending money. When we disagree with them, we may drop the issue rather than engage in heated and sometimes messy discussions. In so doing we deny them the privilege of difficult work, limited finances, or challenging relationships by protecting them from having to deal with them. How often do we steer our kids away from a team, play, or choir tryout because we think they won't do well? When we overprotect our children in this way, we are actually doing them a great disservice by expressing our lack of confidence in them—not only in their ability to achieve but in their ability to handle defeat if they don't.

We Overprotect Because We Confuse Hurt and Harm

In order to clarify here, let's explain adversity's effects according to two terms: *hurt* and *harm*. Though the terms represent two types of pain, we often fear them equally—and run from them both.

Hurt is not usually devastating. It causes enough pain to get the attention of the sufferer, and it can work as a vaccination against the risks that indulgent, overprotective parenting imposes.

Hurt can come in the discomfort of difficult schoolwork that requires intensive hours of study or in the poor grades that come from not studying. Hurt may come in the form of rejection from peers for a betrayal of confidence or as discipline from parents for willful irresponsibility. A summer spent mindlessly inputting data into a computer may feel like hurt to a college student who yearns for excitement. A teenager may hurt financially because of mis-spent funds. Yet despite the discomfort of this sort of pain, an impartial observer can easily see hurt's potential to bless the sufferer of that adversity. Through such hurt the young person can develop a stronger work ethic, relationship skills, self-control, and obedi-ence. That pain can ultimately bless his career motivation, ability to set goals, and fiscal responsibility.

Harm, on the other hand, causes serious damage. No one wants it. Harm can cripple or maim the body, as can happen in car acci-dents, starvation and bulimia through eating disorders, collisions with trees while snowboarding, dives into shallow water, falls over steep cliffs, and violent fights or beatings. Or it can cripple or maim the mind, as it sometimes does with severe neglect; rape; verbal and emotional abuse; drug or alcohol misuse; death, injury, or serious illness of a loved one; addiction to pornography; or victimization from some other crime.

Should we protect our young people and ourselves from such harm? Should we do all we can to avoid it? Absolutely! If we neglect to establish appropriate safeguards and boundaries against such circumstances, we wouldn't be behaving in loving ways toward ourselves or those we care about.

But sometimes rotten events or people do harm us, either directly, when they happen to us or to those we love, or indirectly, when we see, hear, or read about horrors. Whether we experience such horrors personally or vicariously, the excruciating pain can shock and frighten us into a protectiveness that can cause more damage.

Confused by where hurt ends and harm begins, we can lump the two together, because they both cause pain. Unfortunately, then we end up being motivated by pain avoidance, not growth. Because we fear for the child and want to protect her from harm, we end up shielding her from useful hurt at the same time. The result? Risk-riddled overprotection.

Optimal Adversity

When we weigh the difference between hurt and harm, the distinction appears to be one of degree. Aren't we saying that harm is horrible, whereas hurt isn't really so bad? And that telling the difference should be relatively easy? Not necessarily. Evaluating adversity and determining if, when, and how to mitigate its effects is difficult. The answers can vary from child to child. One baby tolerates and adapts to a rigid feeding schedule; another may be injured by it. One child maintains emotional balance during the divorce of her parents; another falls into a deep depression. One teenager thrives in a rigorous academic climate; another may wilt with discouragement in that same setting. Human and environmental variables complicate our assessments and our decision making as we try to choose the best responses to children we care about.

Though we wish adversity pills would go down like vitamins for every child, not all children respond to adversity the same way. Some tolerate high dosages without emotional nausea, whereas others will be bedridden for years. Some grow a strong and healthy character after small to moderate doses, while a few require megadoses of adversity to effect change. Life offers no easy prescriptions.

Doses of adversity our children receive do not always seem tailored to their tolerance or their need. Some kids have been forced to swallow so much pain we think it will kill them. Others don't get enough because we intercept it and flush it away. Sometimes children are injured because of events beyond our control and sometimes because we allow them to endure too little or too much adversity. We make mistakes that cause them pain.

If all adversity simply hurt our kids enough to facilitate character growth and lead them straight to success, we wouldn't fear it so much. But tragedies happen, and they harm our kids terribly.

And yet God tells us that He can turn even the most despicable, devastating harm into something useful, something actually good. Though we can only believe that to the limits of our faith, God is not limited by our lack of faith. If He has allowed a tragedy, then we can be certain that He will translate that pain into an essential ingredient in His loving gift of positive growth. Though we may have trouble grasping love so enormous and powerful that it can eclipse the worst horrors, His love is truly that gigantic, extensive, profound, and magnificent. We stake our lives on the fact that God will not allow a tragedy that He cannot overcome.

Therefore, we who embrace At-Promise thinking can refuse to let those catastrophes destroy us. Though we may need significant time to heal, we believe that we and our children can eventually learn and grow and succeed because of those difficulties. God promises us that this is so in Romans 8:28, if we are only willing to trust Him and listen to Him: "And we know that in all things God works for the good of those who love him, who have been called according to his purpose." Read that passage aloud. Hear the "in *all* things"? No pit we or our children are in is too deep for God to reach us. That means that the God who loves us can transform and redeem any misery, no matter how cruel or traumatic or devastating, into something useful and good.

Well, good for God. I'm glad he thinks my pain has some value. But you know what? I really don't care if God sees it that way, because I don't. I still ache and see no good at all in what happened to me.

I [Cheryl] understand that thinking. When I lost my dad and my mother vented her frustration and anger on us children, I said those words myself. But despite multiple setbacks, I gradually began to let God work through loving people to cultivate promise character in me. And I am still learning. In the process, my heart's eyesight is clearing up. I now recognize how God is using my "temporary" pain (though it lasted for years) for even greater, more enduring good.

Hope-filled interpretations of my memories are crowding out and replacing ugly, hopeless interpretations. For me, as it can be for every person young or old, harm has lost its negative power.

Ways to Help Children Deal with Adversity

How can we help children deal with adversity?

• *We can allow them realistic struggle in the context of solid relationships.* We will benefit children greatly if we model strategies for dealing with the world's curve balls, then encourage those kids to enter the batter's box. Such relationships equip our children with discernment and the confidence with which to swing the bat. Even more, if they strike out, they have the confidence to once again step up to the plate in the next inning.

I [Tim] wanted my son to be successful, so I faked it. I rigged each one-on-one soccer game with my seven-year-old, Tyler. He would end up scoring the winning goal within seconds of every game's end. We celebrated and cheered his successes.

I had always assumed that Tyler knew that I actually had something to teach him about the sport that had consumed most of my youth. However, my boy's three-year winning streak against me had made him world champion in his own mind. The endless stories of my college soccer experiences seemed to have no rebalancing effect. He was clearly untouchable.

I won the next game 9 to 1. Tyler stomped off the field, refusing to play with me anymore.

This might have been the last game we ever played together. That thought scares me. But because I have spent time building a positive and caring relationship with my son, I could instead give Tyler some important, painful reality. Unfortunately, too many parents give in to their fear and refuse to expose their sons and daughters to the failure that helps them develop an appropriate concept of self.

These days Tyler and I are back on the field. I still make sure he wins a fair share of our games, but I have introduced some new variables to our play: loss, struggle, and a good dose of reality about his current but developing abilities. Now when his 205-pound father comes charging down the field with the ball, I can almost see him strategizing how to stop me. He knows now that I might *not* trip over my own feet before making the winning goal. Now Tyler has learned skills and resolve that can catch me off guard as he charges me and goes after the ball. I shudder when I think of being checked (and possibly injured) by him someday during a father-son homecoming game.

In retrospect I see how I weakened my son's resilience by coddling his self-esteem on the soccer field. At the first sign of adversity, he folded. Then I almost overwhelmed him with sudden adversity. Because I realized (even if somewhat clumsily) the need for realistic adversity and had the strength of relationship with my son to fall back on, he is growing. Now, as I introduce adversity into our games, I see in him a stronger desire to win than ever before. He used to assume that he was going to win, as if it were as much a given as his eye color. Now he works hard to win. He wants to learn from me. He asks for lessons because he wants to improve. His determination amazes me as he analyzes our games play by play and plans his next improvements.

• *We can process adversity in front of and with our children.* Another way to help children develop strategies for dealing with adversity is to allow them to watch us and participate with us as we resolve adverse circumstances. This is not easy to do and requires us to be humble and vulnerable with our children. We are tempted to hole ourselves up in a cave while our inner or outer storms blast us. After all, we know that we may not be the most likable when up against a challenge that tests our limits. We do not want to give our young friends free tickets to a show that we would rather avoid ourselves.

But if we disappear (either physically or emotionally) when we are hurting, only to reappear when the storm blows over and the difficult work is finished, we deny children the chance to view the healthy processes for dealing with adversity that we are cultivating. No, we won't always handle things perfectly, but we are learning and growing, making wise decisions and apologizing when we don't, evaluating and planning so that next time we'll handle our trials even more effectively.

Several years ago I [Tim] participated in an Austrian Alps trek that culminated at Schiechen Spitzer, an 8,800-foot peak in the Dachstein mountain range. The final ascent took us two days with an overnight stay in an alpine hut. Though I had climbed a little bit before, I had never joined an expedition that would summit a mountain of this altitude. I found that the confidence to conquer this peak did not rest in the iron bolts drilled into the rock but in the person who climbed ahead of me up the rocky face. Every move she made, I imitated. Every handhold she took was the one I took.

That climber in front of me struggled just as hard as I to climb this mountain. She placed her feet in the footholds chosen by the person in front of her. In this manner the entire team of twenty made it to the top roped together, whereas none of us would have made it to the top alone.

I wish I could say that the summit yielded a glorious view of the Austrian Alps, but it did not. It was a fog-shrouded, cold, windy peak. However, it did reveal that I could learn a lot by watching the person ahead of me, even if she learned to overcome the challenge just moments before it became mine.

We can do the same for the children in our lives by letting them in on our own difficult climbs.

• *We can tell them about our experiences with adversity and help them interpret their own adversity.* If we do our best to recount our stories of adversity with integrity and insight, they can strengthen our children's understanding. As mentors, each of us can act as a narrator in a child's life by foreshadowing trouble; explaining twists in life's plot; and making sense of beginnings, endings, and the conflicts in between.

Though we may fear becoming pretty boring or unlikable storytellers in the midst of our own pain, we can help the kids around us find their way through future suffering by our example, however imperfect. Anne Lamott's words about the relationship between writer and reader might just as easily fit the relationship between parent and child. She says that we sometimes

> turn out to be not all that funny or articulate, but [we] can still be great friends or narrators . . . if [we] have survived or are in the process of surviving a great deal. This is inherently interesting . . . since it is the task in front of all of [them]: sometimes we have to have one hand on this rock here, one hand on that one, and each big toe seeking out firm, if temporary footing, and while we're scaling that rock, there's no time for bubbles, champagne, and a witty aside. [They] don't mind that people in this situation are not being charming. [They] are glad to see [us] doing something [they] will do down the line, and with dignity. The challenge and the dignity make it interesting enough.[11]

Halfway There!

Trials and adversity can be messy and drawn out. They often bring out the worst in children and adults alike. They test relationships, reveal the true self, and inspire tantrums. They also spark conflict, create confusion, and lead us to the edge of our endurance, which is why our natural tendency is to keep children from experiencing them.

In fact, as we've mentioned before, our tendency as parents and educators is to see children who experience adversity, difficulties, and failures as starting from a disadvantaged position in life. We assume they live in the basement well below ground level and must struggle to get above ground first before they can ever begin to climb toward a measure of success. But is this true? Does adversity put kids in a deficit position among their peers?

Picture a child's success like a bank account. To believe that adversity disadvantages a child is to assume that every time a child fails, hurts, or loses, his account balance decreases. Following this logic, the kid with great adversity is left with a severely overdrawn account, with charges and late fees accruing daily. It seems that only a chain of certain successes and positive experiences can reverse the dismal balance.

But what if every time a child experiences pain and adversity, he is making a deposit, not a withdrawal, in his account? What if every time a trusted adult helps him interpret his struggles positively, the balance grows with interest? Then children hurt by family dynamics, overwhelmed by a new language and culture, or trapped by a series of negative choices no longer need to catch up. They are already halfway there.

The At-Promise paradigm, if we take it seriously, can transform the way we counsel, teach, discipline, and mentor the children in our care. If we truly believe that pain and adversity are essential components in a child's positive development, then we no longer need at-risk terminology. All of the factors that traditionally place children at risk are now building blocks of promise. Enfolded by relationship, children's deficits turn into deposits.

Remember . . .

- Adversity provides a catalyst for a child's character growth and is essential to success.

- When we overprotect our children, we are actually doing them a great disservice by expressing our lack of confidence in them—not only in their ability to achieve but in their ability to handle defeat if they don't.

- Though we wish adversity pills would go down like vitamins for every child, not all children respond to adversity the same way.

- In the same way, children must experience resistance in order to grow. When we remove opportunities for them to struggle, we restrict the full development of their innate promise.

Chapter Five

Trust Between a Caring Adult and a Child

To develop normally, children need to be
emotionally nourished by the trustworthy adults
around them.

—*Drew Pinsky, M.D.*

The year is 1976. The place: a town in France, where my [Tim's] family lived, and I attended a local public school with my brother and two sisters. My first-grade teacher was a magnetic guy. I liked him, so I was glad when he invited me to join an exclusive after-school club with several other boys. He coached us for soccer tournaments. He invited us over to his house for chocolate sandwiches. He showed us films like *Pinocchio* and spent lots of time just hanging out with us and making us feel special. My parents liked him and trusted him as a teacher.

One day in class, that same teacher asked me to stop talking to a classmate across the aisle. I refused to obey him and went on talking. Much to my surprise, he walked over to me, picked me up, and placed me in front of the class on top of his desk. He then asked the entire class to stand and applaud me for my defiance of his authority!

For some odd reason, my father did not have the same positive response when I defied him at dinner that night. But my attitude made sense to him during a subsequent parent-teacher conference, when my teacher confidently told my parents that he was grooming me to be a great American Marxist revolutionary. My parents had not realized that my hero was the president of the local Marxist political party. The cartoon movies he was showing me were Soviet propaganda films. Pinocchio became a bad boy in the movie when two shady characters, a rat named Capitalism and a fox named Democracy, led him astray. Later in the movie, the world to which the rat and fox introduced him abandoned Pinocchio. I can still see a Jewish rabbi, a Catholic priest, and Uncle Sam turning their backs on Pinocchio when the boy asked them to save his father, Geppetto, who was lost at sea. Twenty-five years later, I can still remember the story in indelible color.

Within two weeks my parents had withdrawn me from his class and enrolled me in a Catholic school (where two nuns tried to turn me into a priest, but that's another story).

Was my parents' intervention drastic? I don't think so. Their action realigned my relationship with them so that I was submitting to their authority. They, and not a misguided Marxist, once again became my primary influence. It showed their understanding of the powerful influence that adults can have in the lives of children.

As with any force in nature, the influential power an adult can extend into the life of a child can build up—or destroy—that child. Have no doubt: some adult will influence the child you care about. The question therefore becomes not "Will our children have significant relationships with adults?" but "With whom will our children have significant relationships?"

We have a great responsibility to be discerning about the adults who mentor our young people. Before placing kids on the community soccer team or in an after-school program, we must take the time to get to know the influencers in their lives. Simply put, we must screen opportunities for relationships.

Grant Fiedler, the man who recruited me [Tim] into school administration and became a mentor to me during my first years of boarding school leadership, offered me the best litmus test for hiring teachers. He said, "When in doubt, there is only one question to ask; 'Would I want this person teaching my child?' If I can answer 'Yes!' without hesitation, then I offer that teacher a contract." Grant understands that people, not polished résumés or glowing references, influence children.

AT-PROMISE PRINCIPLE 2: A trusting relationship with a caring adult helps a child interpret adversity and develop promise character.

We are relational creatures. We live in community. We learn better in groups. We prefer playing with other people, and we may feel silly when we hear the restaurant hostess say, "Party of one?" Dr. Arthur Holmes, professor of philosophy at Wheaton College in Illinois, suggests that a child's identity is "relationally rooted" because he or she exists "in relation to God in and through other relationships."[1] God created us to need relationship. That's perhaps why God employs a trusting relationship to develop promise character. Immeasurable power is unleashed when a caring adult invests time, energy, and loving discipline in the life of a child. The effects of this power are undeniable and clearly documented through research.[2]

Even in infancy a trusting relationship with a caregiver is critical. Without that relationship emotional development is arrested. Having already raised four other children, my [Cheryl's] sister and brother-in-law, Jan and Chris Soto, brought three siblings who struggle with reactive attachment disorder into their home. Up until the children were one, two, and three, their birth mother had often left them alone in an apartment to fend for themselves—for up to a week at a time. They ate crackers, Cheerios, whatever food they could scrounge up, but they were hungry—for both physical and emotional food. When a social worker brought the kids to Jan and Chris, the children had never bonded to their mother—or to anyone. They had already learned that they couldn't trust anyone to meet their needs and that if they cried, no one would care.

According to Terry Levy and Michael Orlans, in *Attachment, Trauma, and Healing,* babies who have their needs soothed and met repeatedly by the same caregiver learn to trust, and they bond to that person. Once a child has bonded, he will be capable of bonding to others, and emotional development can continue. But if the caregiver regularly neglects or treats the baby unkindly when he needs attention, he learns that he cannot depend on adults. He will have trouble forming secure attachments to anyone. Later that mistrust will translate into a desperate need to control; he will think his survival depends on being in charge. Unless someone who understands the disorder intervenes and shows him how to reciprocate in a relationship of trust, his original trauma will damage his relationships for the rest of his life.[3] What a desperate prognosis!

But relationship can help even these terribly injured children succeed, as Jan and Chris know. The neglected kids who arrived at their home as preschoolers seven years ago are slowly learning to trust their parents and to surrender some of the control and rage so common to kids with their early childhood experiences. They can stick with some tasks now and sometimes admit when they are wrong. Jan sees sparks of optimism in them and of hope. They tell the truth more and sneak less. And sometimes they play with carefree abandon.

Change is painfully gradual and setbacks regular, but Jan and Chris have hope for these kids. They firmly believe that their committed relationships with their children will make a difference. Having heard that children with reactive attachment disorder statistically have tremendous risk of failure, I [Cheryl] asked Chris if he thought any of the kids they had known were too damaged to reach. "Yes," he said. I looked back at him blankly. Then he continued:

> Their traumas have even changed the physiology of their brains. We do all we can, but their injuries are often more serious than our capabilities can address. I'd be lying if I didn't say we'd been tempted to give up.
>
> But how can we? Many times we have been surprised. We can't predict when some healing or growth will happen—or in which child. Sometimes the one we least expect to respond will let trust into the hole in his broken heart. Jan and I have recognized that our job is to take care of these kids as faithfully as we can and then watch God work. The results aren't up to us.

Educational research consistently demonstrates that children who have a positive relationship with their parents or with another caring adult are more likely to be successful in school and in life than are children who do not have that relationship.[4] These positive relationships—whether with a parent, aunt, uncle, grandparent, teacher, neighbor, formal or informal mentor, employer, coach, or youth group leader—act as appropriate protectors against some of life's hazards, including poverty and abuse, and can serve as interpreters of pain and adversity, which every child will naturally encounter.[5]

When Billy "Z" Zeoli, former White House chaplain, walked into Don Eller's life, Don was in a lot of trouble. He had been in and out of jail since he was seventeen years old. He had seven drunk-driving charges and came close to being indicted on charges related to fraud that would probably have sent him to federal prison. Although Don had given up on himself, Billy saw something in him that no one else was willing or able to see. As Don puts it, "Billy put me under his wing, and that's where I've stayed. He keeps me on the straight. He is a great mentor, and I've been hanging with him ever since."

Don now works for Billy Zeoli and Gospel Communications International, where he serves as coordinator of Project Free Forever, a jail ministry reaching out to inmates across the state of Michigan.

Did Don deserve Billy's commitment to him? Not on your life. Nonetheless, Billy was willing to offer Don a completely unearned, undeserved relationship with him, through which Billy loved, mentored, and held Don accountable. Why? Because Billy saw Don from an At-Promise perspective. He extended grace to Don because of who Don was, not because of what he had done or not done. Billy did not reach out to Don because he thought he should but because he genuinely had hope for him. He saw him as a child whom God had created with wonderful potential for success. He believed, even when Don himself didn't, that Don could become a success; he trusted that as Don's character grew, he would become capable of contributing positively to the fabric of society. And he has!

The At-Promise perspective eclipses risk without denying it. It allows us to see a child of any age as a caterpillar wrapped in a constricting cocoon and as an airborne butterfly simultaneously. It makes us stake our lives on the fact that more is going on inside that shabby, gray chrysalis than meets the ordinary eye, because we see what a child is and is becoming all at the same time. Billy Zeoli certainly recognized the risky patterns and behaviors in Don Eller's life, but he refused to let them label Don or consign him to a future of failure. He looked beyond the risk to Don's innate promise and inherent potential. When we develop At-Promise eyesight like Billy's, we can begin counting butterflies before they hatch and convincing earthbound caterpillars that they will fly.

Programs Need Relationships

We live in a culture of outsourcing responsibilities. Because we lack time or capability ourselves, we outsource jobs as the most efficient way to get tasks done. If we work outside the home and can afford it, we hire a housecleaner. We let Federal Express ship our packages and Charles Schwab handle our mutual funds. Too often adults also outsource relationships with children, expecting school programs and extracurricular activities to build kids' character whether we are involved or not.

Most of us agree that children need positive and caring relationships with adults. We also agree that these relationships contribute significantly to a child's success. Even so, we regularly scapegoat our schools, churches, and sports programs by passing the buck of responsibility for our young people. We say that we believe in relationships but rely instead on programs to fill the gaps. Having seen or heard about young lives changed as a result of participating in mentoring and discipleship programs, we mistakenly attribute the success to the programs themselves.

Programs alone don't change children, however. The catalyst for a child's metamorphosis lies in the relationship between a trusted mentor and child, not in the program that initiated that connection. We celebrate programs offered throughout the country that understand this concept and that emphasize caring relationships. Numerous national, regional, and local programs base their mission on the importance of one-to-one relationships.

However, though educational research points to the benefits of a caring relationship between an adult and child, the majority of our public and private schools still look for programmatic solutions to their problems rather than creating opportunities for children to connect with adults they can trust.

Some after-school tutoring programs demonstrate this problem. Children rotate between tutors on schedule rather than meeting with the same tutor on a regular basis. While these programs certainly have their value and can help a child's academic performance, what remedial children really need is a positive relationship with an adult, a relationship that a tutoring program facilitates. See the difference? People, not programs, inspire growth. Programs may offer one road to success, but people are the vehicle.

Any adults hoping to guide children toward success would be wise to choose not just exceptional programs but programs based upon the exceptional relationships children can develop through them.

A nationwide study from the Lutheran Brotherhood and Search Institute revealed that even though most adults have a good idea of what children need from them, they do not act on their own beliefs. This study looked at adult involvement in the lives of kids outside their immediate family and showed that just one in twenty adults is actively involved in a child's positive development.[6]

Young People Want Relationship

Today's young people are calling out for relationship. A recent survey revealed that 84 percent of teens said that their "future success" depends upon whether they have "close family relationships."[7] Contrary to popular belief, studies have also shown that high school students name their parents as the most "significant" adults in their lives.[8] It is time for parents, educators, and youth workers to contribute to what we know will make a meaningful difference in the lives of the next generation. We can build trusting, "family like" relationships with them.

The At-Promise Difference

Let's first look at what the At-Promise relationship between adult and child is not. The child is not a project, nor is she or he someone toward whom an adult tosses encouragement and pep talks without follow-up, honest interaction, instruction, and self-revelation. It was not enough for Billy Zeoli to tell Don Eller that he saw promise in him. Though altering language can indeed help alter people, simply replacing the at-risk label with an At-Promise epithet is not enough. Just as Billy needed to enter into a trusted relationship of accountability with Don in order to influence his life, so too do we need to act upon the promise we see in the child, the promise we voice. Words become most powerful when they become flesh. When we translate our spoken blessings toward kids into action, children will begin to trust our words; then positive change will occur.

I [Tim] remember sitting through several Wheaton College chapel talks in which internationally recognized speakers hailed us students as "the leadership of our generation." If they could have eavesdropped on my thoughts, they would have heard me thinking, *How can you say that? You don't even know me!* I did not want to be "knighted" by people who didn't know my name, who didn't know that most of the time my fellow students and I were just bungling along in that esteemed college setting. I wanted to hear authentic prophecy about my promise from those who interacted with me regularly, who could see me as I was and still anticipate my success.

Young people can sniff out empty promises and cure-all potions before the stoppers are off the bottles. They do not want words alone. Kids may grow weary of adult acquaintances telling them that they have potential. They often don't believe them and instead quietly think, *If you really knew me, you wouldn't say that.*

A Calling

If the At-Promise perspective is more than words, what does it look like? An At-Promise relationship is one to which we caring adults are called. God sets a child in the life of an adult whose heart He is preparing to recognize the promise in that child. We may be called to relationship with only two or three children in our entire lifetimes, or God may call us to many more. Although we may meet the child through a formally arranged mentoring situation, we are just as likely to sense a calling to a child in our neighborhood; at family gatherings; through connections with school, clubs, church, work, or hobbies; or even (and especially) in our own home. Regardless of how the relationship begins, when we spend time with children to whom we are called, we can't help but see a bright future for them. We don't worry that they may not yet see that same promise, but when we see it, that's our call.

A few months ago, I [Cheryl] was unloading the dishwasher when the phone rang and Debbie Lewey Stallcup greeted me. Did I remember her? She wasn't sure I would. On the contrary, memories from twenty-six years before in the tiny town of Colfax, Washington, jumped to life, and I pictured Debbie Lewey, then my student at Colfax High School, plain as day.

"I'm just calling to say thanks," she began, "for what you did for me. You saved my life, you know." I sat down, astonished. I didn't know.

"What do you mean?" I queried, certain that age was claiming my recollections. Had I pulled her from the bottom of a swimming pool? Performed a Heimlich maneuver on her in the school cafeteria? I scanned my mental archives and found nothing. I had no idea what she was talking about. For three years I had known the teenage Debbie. She had attended my classes and performed in two plays I directed. We had talked often. Back then Debbie was spunky, athletic, irrepressible, hard-working, and ran with a wild crowd. Rumor had it that she had endured very difficult family circumstances, though she only occasionally talked about her home life and then only offered me glimpses.

I didn't pry, but I did enjoy spending time with her. Debbie was fun, honest, and trustworthy. Couched in her tough, strong persona, I saw a tenderness and unselfishness that delighted me and drew me to her. So when I needed a dependable employee for our small business, I immediately thought of Debbie. She worked for me until my husband finished graduate school and we left the area. No matter how challenging her assignment, she met and exceeded my expectations.

Her voice brought me back to my kitchen nearly three decades later. "You made a difference more than you know. You heard about my brother, didn't you?"

I had heard. Her older brother had died of a drug overdose nearly thirteen years earlier. "His death wasn't accidental, Cheryl. He just couldn't take the pain anymore." I waited while she told a story of abuse and violence during their childhood years that broke my heart. "If not for you, I would have followed in his footsteps. I'm sure I'd be dead. We hurt so badly and could never tell anyone how desperate our lives really were. I learned to be tough, to cover what I was feeling. I dodged relationships with adults, so teachers didn't like me. None of them thought I would ever do much. Until you."

I protested. Surely they had seen Debbie's wonderful potential! Yes, she had some rough edges and didn't put serious stock in academics, but I saw her as an amazing girl. Her promise eclipsed her blemishes. I genuinely believed she could do anything. Apparently, I had told her so all those years ago, then offered her trust and friendship to back up my words. I don't remember, but she does.

"I succeeded because of you," she said. "When you offered me that job, I was so surprised that you asked me. I wanted to succeed because you trusted me. Later, though no one believed I would finish college, I just knew I could. In 1990 I finished my master's in education, with a specialty in counseling. For the last twenty-three years, I have worked with kids in trouble—the ones they call 'high risk,' ones in lockup, inpatient, outpatient. Now I work with juvenile probation. I've served on the Idaho Governor's Children-at-Risk Task Force through two governors. Even chaired it for two years."

I was thrilled at Debbie's success. For decades she has been contributing positively to society's moral and social fabric.

She continued: "I have your picture up in my office. I show it to the kids I work with and tell them that when someone believes in you, you can do anything."

We talked awhile more about the accumulated events of the intervening years before we said good-bye. I hung up, teary and full of gratitude that I had had the privilege of loving her.

I was also astonished that my small efforts had made such a difference for her. Nothing I did was heroic or remarkable. Caring about Debbie was easy. I liked her and *wanted* to spend time with her, though they were just snippets of time over the course of three years. At-Promise relationships often work like that. They develop as naturally as breathing, if we just don't hold our breath.

But sometimes we do hold our breath. Sometimes we see an At-Promise child, and then the fear rolls in. To be free enough and love-filled enough to spot the promise in the child to whom we are called, we must first allow love to deactivate the fears that keep us from seeing past a child's present condition. Those fears can short-circuit our awareness of the connection we could have with him or her.

If I had believed the opinions of those who couldn't see Debbie's promise, if I had kept her at arm's length because of her toughness or incorrectly perceived social behaviors, if I had been afraid of how much time she would take, I'd have missed the opportunity of knowing her and of learning how God worked through our relationship. What if I had chosen to fear that I couldn't be a friend to Debbie? What if I had thought myself too different, too boring, too old, too young, or too inept to build a relationship with her? We would both have missed out on a relationship that blessed us.

Instead, because God called us together and opened my eyes to her promise, I could love her both as she was right then and as I trusted she could be. My vision for her future took on its own unique, God-inspired shape. Then, in the wonderful At-Promise way, because I naturally had hope for her, she did too.

If we want to spot a child's promise, we do need to pay attention and concentrate gently on the young people we encounter. Sometimes seeing a child from the At-Promise perspective is a little like looking at one of those Magic Eye three-dimensional pictures, the ones that drive you crazy until you can see the picture hidden in a complicated illustration. In order to see the buried picture clearly, you must focus your eyes to simultaneously see it and see past it, as if you were also looking at a distant point through and beyond the picture. If you focus too much on the immediate illustration, you will miss the picture's buried beauty, which only emerges when you look at it and beyond it with alert but "soft" eyes.

Just when family and friends are chuckling at your frustration, and just when you are about to give up hope of ever seeing the picture emerge, the art comes into focus. You wonder how you ever missed it, why you couldn't see it all along.

Many adults who care deeply about children are going cross-eyed trying to see a child's promise. We suspect that God's fine art is hidden beneath the jumbled images of pierced bodies, tattoos, and pink hair; beneath a facade of invincible, excellent performance; or beneath dark, scowling pain. That art may resemble Rembrandt or may be more akin to Picasso, but when we see it, we will have an At-Promise picture of the child we care about. And you know what's great? Those three-dimensional experiences are hard to reverse. Once you see the promise, you will always see it, though you may be the only person who sees the present and future promise in that particular child.

That's why the At-Promise relationship is a calling. If you see the promise, you must trust that you are called to act on it in whatever way you can. Go to the level you are comfortable. Don't force it. Give what you can.

Inspired by Grace

Next, an At-Promise relationship is grace-filled. The student doesn't earn the love and time we offer her. We want to build relationship with her not because of what she does but because of who she is: a child created in the image of God and filled with promise from birth. Our relationship is based on grace: an unmerited, free gift, something we want to offer, not a duty we grudgingly feel we have to fulfill. It's not forced but is natural, like mine [Cheryl's] was with Debbie. Though we don't always expect it to be easy (and it may not be!), we look forward to spending time with the child, and we often enjoy ourselves.

If you think the grace in an At-Promise relationship is looking a little like God's grace, His free gift of acceptance, to us, well, you've caught the vision! We can love kids just as they are because God loves us just as we are—flawed, incomplete, and with much growing yet to do. When He gives you or me the magic eyes to see the promise in a child, God is calling us to love that child the way He loves us—unconditionally, joyfully, and hopefully. His magic eyes see us that way.

And what about the results of our efforts with these kids? Don't worry about them. They are up to God, not us. One thing is certain: love always bears good fruit, though we may not even hear about it for twenty-six years.

Relationship Can Happen at Any Time

As we began studying At-Promise relationships, we tried to identify parameters for when and how they develop. Just when we naively thought we could define the scope and range of At-Promise interactions, we would hear about another connection that broke every definition we'd come up with. That's because there are no concrete definitions. At-Promise relationships don't all look the same. They can happen several times throughout a young person's life—or only once. A five-year-old or a thirty-five-year-old "child" may be profoundly influenced by such mentorship. A trusted connection with a caring adult may be brief (spanning a week in a summer-camp setting) or enduring (lasting an entire lifetime).

But whatever the circumstances or duration, At-Promise relationships between young people and caring adults offer children hope:

- By giving them insight into their At-Promise identity
- By modeling and encouraging character growth that leads to success
- By imparting a greater understanding of how to interpret and respond to the adversity in their lives

I [Tim] recently spoke with Dr. Robert Schuller, the founder and pastor of the Crystal Cathedral in Garden Grove, California. Dr. Schuller's positive message of hope has encouraged thousands of individuals around the world to place their faith in God and reach beyond what they ever dreamed possible. I wanted to hear his story, the story of a farm boy from Iowa who has encouraged so many people in his lifetime. What surprised me about his story was how young he was when the words of a bold uncle offered him hope and direction, ultimately confirming his destiny. His experience captures yet another example of the power that one caring individual can have over a child without knowing the lasting significance his words and actions will have.

Robert's childhood resembled that of other boys in his Dutch farming neighborhood. Hard work and poverty were staples in the community's diet. The Ten Commandments were foundational law, and kids minded their elders if they knew what was best for them.

When Robert's missionary uncle returned from China on furlough, he spent time with the Schullers. One day Uncle Henry put his hand on the small boy's head and said directly to him, "You're going to be a preacher when you grow up."

As Dr. Schuller tells it today, "He challenged me. He announced it as if he saw the vision. I took it as an absolute." The rest is history. Dr. Schuller's story is that of a young boy who accepted his At-Promise identity at an early age because a believing uncle was bold enough to speak promise into his life. Many of life's obstacles and barriers could have deterred Dr. Schuller, but they didn't. From that moment on, he never doubted the preacher he was in the process of becoming. The power that our words and presence have over children is hard to grasp but both cautionary and inspiring once we understand.

The Ultimate Relationship

Nancy, Carol, Andrea, and I [Cheryl] were driving to the Fragrance Lake trailhead for a morning's hike when I asked them to identify a pivotal, transforming time in their lives, when something happened that plunged them into a time of character growth and insight. Three of us remembered times when pain we had experienced began to make sense and when we began to grow because of it. And for all three of us, a significant relationship with a trusted adult initiated that growth—and fed it.

But not for Andrea. Though she had grown up with a mentally ill mother in a chaotic home, years had seen her transformed. Though educators had labeled her as an at-risk child expected to fail, she has matured into a stable, wise, loving mother, mentor, church volunteer, and community advocate.

"I didn't have any mentors," she told us. "I didn't get close to anyone. My mom was crazy, and us six kids overwhelmed my poor dad. He spent all his energy running the farm and seeing that we were clothed and fed when Mom was having bad spells. He never knew what Mom would do next, and caring for her preoccupied him. So our relationships with him and others were distant at best. There was such a stigma attached to mental illness in those days that few folks came around. And the only place Dad ever took us was to church."

Then it dawned on her. "You know, I did meet someone at church whom I ignored for a long time before I listened to him. So I guess I agree. Relationship did set my growth in motion."

"Who was it?" Carol asked. "Some guy at youth group?"

Andrea tossed her head back and laughed. "Way better," she said. "I finally said yes to God." We understood. For each of us, relationship with the Lord has been the ultimate relationship of trust.

Calvin Theological Seminary Professor Ronald Nydam writes,

> People change as the result of relationships, most importantly their relationship with Jesus Christ . . . because they are loved; the Word becomes flesh and dwells among us by the power of the Holy Spirit. People in pain find hope because we have hope. The young take on the values of their parents because they are loved by their parents. People feel understood, and the weight of their sorrows is lifted. When we care for others and make these spiritual connections, the emotional bond we develop communicates that a person matters, that he or she is significant. The cared-for-person-in-relationship responds by taking in our hopes, our beliefs, our Lord. This dynamic theory of change is the most "expensive" because we do not simply offer rewards or punishments or even good and right ideas, but we are called to offer ourselves in relationship.[9]

Growth Requires Looking in the Mirror

We cannot give away something that we do not possess. If you have not recently taken an inventory of your character, most children will conduct one for you free of charge. In fact my [Tim's] children regularly display many of my character flaws. As uncomfortable as looking into the mirror can be, children will boldly model the characteristics they see in our lives. It's true: what kids see, they imitate. Therefore, if we want to build At-Promise characteristics into the lives of our children, we must first consider the evidence of character in our own lives.

Let's look once again at the promise characteristics we listed in Chapter One.

- Perseverance
- Responsibility for our actions
- Optimism
- Motivation from identity
- Integrity
- Service
- Engaged play

Do these character traits flourish in your life? Do you acknowledge your weaknesses? Own up to your mistakes? Are you modeling for the children in your care the traits you want them to develop? Not completely? Welcome to the club. We are all in process. As the bumper sticker reads, "Be patient. God isn't finished with me yet."

That's why this is the most important question: Are you willing to commit to your own character growth—so that you can model promise character to children you mentor? When we are willing to honestly assess our own character and then humbly submit ourselves to the process of growth and change, we can increase the possibility of leading young people through adversity to success. The next seven chapters will show the goals and results of that character development.

Reflecting on Our Own At-Promise Relationships

For a child's true At-Promise identity to be sealed, someone must love and care for that child with a vision of her promise—present and future. If we page through our memories, we can easily identify the person or people who did this for us. They probably don't realize the impact they had on our lives, but we know that without their ability to see our promise, we would not be who we are today.

Will you set this book aside for a few minutes and list the people who saw your promise and made a significant impact in your life? Then jot their names below:

1. _____

2. _____

3. _____

4. _____

Now please pick up the phone or a pen and contact each person. Thank that person for the way he or she influenced your life. As I [Tim] was reflecting on those people who encouraged me, I thought of Dr. Cliff Schimmels, one of my Wheaton College professors and one of the most influential people in my life. Just last week I learned that he died last year. I regret that I didn't write to him before he passed away, to let him know the full extent of his influence on my life. His love for children and learning, and the way he believed in my ability to become a great teacher, changed my life course. In many ways this book is a tribute to him. Thank you, Dr. Schimmels.

Only Halfway There!

Young people fortunate enough to have a caring, At-Promise adult in their lives are truly halfway there! Just like the young people described in Chapter Four who suffer adversity's pain, a child with supportive adult relationships is investing in the other half of success. But it is only half. For a child to develop a balanced life portfolio, he needs both people and pain.

We can easily fall into the trap of believing that advantaged children have everything they need to succeed in life. These are sometimes the good kids from good families who have the smarts and are going places. We often believe that if all-star kids don't blow it, they have it made.

But what happens when our all-star kids blow everything? Problems will come. These kids will fall short of expectations and mess up. Often when this happens, we are so quick to despair. Then what messages do we give these kids when they limp into our homes, classrooms, and offices with fresh failures weighing them down? Don't we often communicate that when they mess up, they've fallen from grace and down into the basement?

This is simply not true. Failure that a child experiences while in relationship with a caring adult is an essential component to that child's success. Therefore, we must believe that this experience may be exactly what this child needs to grow. The At-Promise paradigm offers confidence that our positive relationships with young people are not enough. We can never love children out of their pain, only through it.

So what does this mean to those of us who work and live with advantaged kids? How can the At-Promise paradigm offer hope for the good kid who messes up? First of all, we know that relationship is only half the equation. Many of our kids are only halfway there. We also know that at some point every child is going to experience trials, defeats, challenges, and disappointments just like we do. And when this happens, we can look at these hurting kids with hope, knowing that they have just been offered the other part of the equation. In relationship we can help them make sense of adversity and choose to use it on their road to success.

Remember . . .

- A trusting relationship with a caring adult helps a child interpret adversity and develop promise character.
- The act of a caring adult investing time, energy, and loving discipline into the life of a child unleashes immeasurable power.
- The At-Promise perspective eclipses risk without denying it.

It allows us to see a child of any age as a caterpillar wrapped in a constricting cocoon and as an airborne butterfly simultaneously.

- We want to build relationship with her not because of what she does but because of who she is: a child created in the image of God and filled with promise from birth.

- Therefore, if we want to build At-Promise characteristics into the lives of our children, we must first consider the evidence of character in our own lives.

Part Three

Promise Character

At-Promise Principles 3 to 9

Chapter Six

Perseverance

The pearl is the answer of the injured life to that
which injures it.

—*Anonymous*

Mollusks such as oysters and abalone protect their tender bodies
from harm with shells they manufacture from a combination of
aragonite mineral sheets and conchiolin protein. Unless a hungry
predator pries open the shell, that hard exterior keeps the oyster's
soft insides safe. Occasionally, however, a stray food particle gets
trapped inside the shell, irritating that tender tissue. In response the
oyster may coat it with layer after layer of the shell-building mineral and protein. Over time that mollusk transforms the irritant
into a luminous, precious pearl.

AT-PROMISE PRINCIPLE 3: Perseverance empowers us to endure
adversity and sustain hope.

Oysters don't do much thinking. The biological process that
produces a pearl is not a volitional act. Oysters don't decide to persevere. Even so, oysters can teach us a few things about how perseverance produces a beautiful result—a pearl of character that,
when formed in us and the children we love, empowers us to
endure adversity and sustain hope.

Steps to Perseverance

Here's how perseverance, the P in promise character, can develop
in kids:

1. Adversity confronts a young person over time.

2. A trusted adult helps a child respond proactively to the ongoing challenge day after day, perhaps month after month or year after year. That adult explains or demonstrates how to respond to the trial.

3. Eventually the child wraps the painful trials in a new perspective, an understanding that even though he or she may want that adversity gone, it no longer paralyzes as it originally did. The child has learned that solutions are possible but that discovering and implementing them takes persistence. The process has taught the child not to quit. Interpreted adversity has taught the child to persevere.

A Nation of Quitters

Sadly, huge numbers of Americans do not understand how to stick with it for the long haul, either in beliefs or behavior. A significant percentage of our population has made it a habit to throw in the towel instead of persevering. Here are some key statistics on Americans who quit.

- Forty-six states reported 957,200 divorces in the year 2000. This figure does not include California, Colorado, Indiana, and Louisiana—states that do not keep track of divorce numbers.[1] Projections could reasonably estimate well over a million divorces for that year.

- Approximately thirty thousand people committed suicide in the United States in 1999.[2]

- Even with only thirty-six states and the District of Columbia reporting, 371,289 students dropped out of high school in the 1999–2000 school year. (Fourteen states, including our most populous, did not even report their dropouts: Arizona, California, Colorado, Florida, Hawaii, Idaho, Indiana, Kansas, Michigan, New Hampshire, New York, North Carolina, South Carolina, and Washington.)[3]

How many people would have made better choices if they had learned to persevere toward success in the face of trials? Given adversity and trusted, persevering adults to help them make sense of those challenges, wouldn't many of them have chosen differently—both in childhood and in adulthood? Would they have been more likely to stay in their marriages? To finish school? To stay alive? We think so.

Helpless and Hopeless

Dr. Martin Seligman, pioneer researcher of "learned helplessness," studied why people quit. He believes that "only inescapable events produce giving up."[4] In other words when people believe that nothing they do will help them complete school, lessen depression, or heal their marriages, they have bought the lie that they are helpless to succeed.

So what do they do next? They drop out of school, kill themselves, divorce their spouses, or surrender to a defeatist attitude that results in the same mental and relational losses. Either way, they quit. Clearly, statistics and the following story illustrate the fact that not every irritated oyster produces a pearl, despite its potential.

Suffering Requires Perseverance

Jose Bufill, a medical oncologist in South Bend, Indiana, told the story of a young, HIV-positive man who consulted him shortly after Dr. Bufill completed his clinical training. Though the patient exhibited no signs of illness, he asked the doctor if he would help him end his life. Despite the fact that he was still capable of working and living independently, he had lost his will to live and wanted to die as soon as he could arrange it.

Confronted with the pain and difficulties his illness would eventually bring, the young man was ready to quit. He viewed his own euthanasia as a mercy, an attitude that Dr. Bufill considered misguided. He disagreed with his patient's belief that his life was worth living only if he didn't have to suffer and lamented that the young man seemed to find no value in a life colored by suffering.[5]

How often are we like this young patient? How often are we ready to quit on a relationship or a task when we know it will involve suffering and struggle? Will we have the stamina necessary to press on in spite of difficulty?

In Galatians 5 the apostle Paul includes self-control as one of the Holy Spirit's fruits. That trait of managing mind, body, emotions, time, and direction is produced by—and produces—perseverance. Children rarely stumble onto this attribute. Instead, they develop it when adversity demands it of them. Although some children have stubborn enough temperaments to persevere through some trials, a child has a much greater likelihood of developing the trait if an adult who has learned to persevere can support and encourage the child through hard times. Successful people persevere.

Generational Endurance

Many of you have made it through excruciating, exhausting adversity. Maybe you have believed that your adversity was useless, your pain barren. Experience tells us otherwise. When we persevere through pain and emerge on the other side of that dark experience, we can offer hope and instruction to young people and others around us.

Lori Reinsma Fransen's brother Brent fell from a roof while on a construction job and died when Lori was twenty years old. He left behind a heartbroken family, who hated what had happened and grieved intensely for him. Even so, Lori's parents, Bill and Karen, would not allow the tragedy to splinter their family or destroy their hope in God. Although mired in pain, they persevered in their faith and in their unconditional love and support for each other. As Lori remembers, they nourished their other children, ranging in age from ten to twenty-one, as well as Brent's wife and baby girls. They committed themselves to sustaining a close-knit family life, despite loss so profound it could have driven a wedge between them all.

Then in May 1997, Lori, by then a wife and mother, took her toddler, Bryce, to his pediatrician for a routine examination. The results, however, were anything but routine. Wilms' tumor, a malignant tumor of the kidney, was consuming the tiny boy's body. Despite difficult surgeries and chemotherapy, Bryce died at home in his dad's arms two years later.

Is anyone really prepared for a child to die? "No," says Lori. But God used the long vigil with grief she had endured years earlier alongside her parents to help equip her to endure Bryce's long illness. When Bryce died, that was all Lori could do—endure. Friends could see her grief. Lori hunched her shoulders, bowing them in a shield to protect her heart from further pain.

On an early June evening nearly two years after Bryce's death, my running partner, Cindy, called me [Cheryl]. "Lori wants to run in the Seattle Half-Marathon," she said. "In Bryce's memory. It benefits cancer research. What do ya think? Wanna come?"

I shivered involuntarily, then grumbled. The race was in late November, a month of blustery, frigid rainstorms in western Washington.

Cindy ignored my complaints. "The way I see it, Lori has three challenges," she continued. "She had a C-section eight weeks ago, is nursing, and hasn't run distances before."

No, only two challenges, I thought, remembering Bryce. *Lori has run the longest distance. We'll do well if we can keep up with her.* "Sure. Worth a try," I said.

We three met at Lori's the next day, Cindy packing a calendar outlining the training that she and Lori had begun the previous Monday. Lori—sleep-deprived and with sore, leaking breasts—struggled to jog longer than two minutes but refused to quit.

Each week thereafter, we ran incrementally more and walked less. One day in mid-July, we ran for thirty minutes (about three miles) nonstop. Lori, who no longer checked the stopwatch every hundred feet, slapped our upraised palms in celebration.

And she had a lot of palms to slap, high fives for a dozen women who had joined the group over the preceding weeks. One by one we had come alongside Lori, hoping to encourage her, to run with her through her healing. Little did any of us realize how much God would encourage us through our fellowship with each other and through Lori's example. The girl knew how to persevere.

Why did we run with Lori? After all, we were an ordinary, busy group of women, aged thirty-two to forty-eight, with thirty-three children between us. We were involved in our churches and communities, and we worked at a variety of careers from homemaking to teaching to accounting. Why then did so many of us take time to run together?

Because like all ordinary people, we knew the pain of this damaged world. One of us grew up with a chronically ill mother. A drunk driver put another in a three-week-long coma while she was pregnant with her firstborn. We have, like Lori, buried brothers: one with cancer, another with AIDS. Three of our fathers have died. The grade-school daughter of one of us suffers from a debilitating autoimmune disease. Some of us have lived with alcoholism, anxiety, divorce, diabetes, and depression. And we have grieved for Bryce.

That's why we kept running. For Lori. For each other. We could because, with the support of loved ones, we had successfully limped and struggled and cried and raged and prayed our way through pain. In so doing we had cultivated the self-discipline necessary to persevere patiently.

We knew that Lori needed us—and we needed each other—to get through the tough training ahead. We had learned firsthand the Bible's truth that Lori's parents had taught her years before: "Two are better than one. . . . If one falls down, his friend can help him up. . . . Though one may be overpowered . . . a cord of three strands is not quickly broken" (Ecclesiastes 4:10, 12). Just as friends and family had supported all of us through our earlier trials, we trusted that this new rope of sisters would haul us all the way to the end of the race, where we could relax, laugh, and celebrate!

Through our earlier pain, we had come to know that "suffering produces perseverance; perseverance, character; and character, hope" (Romans 5:3–5). Consequently, on pitch-black, predawn training runs, with bodies crying for rest, we could jog alongside Lori with hope. When we suffered aches and fatigue, we anticipated the joy of completing the race.

By September we were boosting mileage. In October we reached eleven miles; by early November, twelve. When the drizzly race day arrived, Lori set the pace for all 13.1 miles. We watched out for each other as we ran, slowing when someone faltered on tough hills, nudging each other into water stops. We talked and joked as we plodded along, in order to take our minds off our groaning joints and puffing lungs and to help each other focus on the hope braided into the pain of it all. When we turned the corner into Seattle's Memorial Stadium, we gripped each other's hands and crossed the finish line together. Relationship and adversity had taught us to persevere.

Persevering in Faith

As we showed in Chapter Five, a relationship with God is the most significant caring relationship a young person can have. Scripture tells us what happens when adversity challenges that relationship of faith: "Consider it pure joy, my brothers, when you face trials of many kinds, because you know that the testing of your faith develops perseverance. Perseverance must finish its work so that you may be mature and complete, not lacking anything" (James 1:2–4). See how the At-Promise paradigm works? Adversity interpreted by a caring adult can help a child develop perseverance—a precursor to maturity, completeness, and success.

In a broken world, where no human being will escape adversity, God doesn't waste our pain. Nothing can happen to us, nothing is so severe that He cannot overcome it with good. Whether in this generation or the next, this life or the next, our—and our children's—suffering, no matter how heinous, will be redeemed, will be used for a greater good if we'll choose to persist in our faith and to trust our loving God with the outcome.

Randy and Jan De Boer and their kids attend the same church our [Cheryl's] family does. Randy was our daughter's fifth-grade teacher, and my husband helped coach their son Matt's high school golf team. As a high school senior, Matt was one of my students. He and our son have been best friends for years. Our families' lives have intertwined regularly, and we have grown to love their family.

So when Randy suffered a seizure this summer, and resulting tests located a brain tumor, we reeled, prayed, and wept. Surgeons removed the tumor successfully and sent it to the lab for analysis. Even harder news followed: the tumor was *glioblastoma multiforme*, a nasty cancer that seeds itself in the brain like a tossed handful of sand. Now Randy is traveling to the hospital five days a week for radiation treatments. And he's receiving chemotherapy.

His prognosis? Well, we don't know when Randy will be healed, but we do know that he will be healed, if not in this lifetime, then after it. In the meantime he is succeeding mightily. Randy, you see, refuses to quit. In the midst of potentially nauseating and fatiguing treatments, he continues to teach his students almost every day. His goal, he told me, is "to be productive and positive . . . the most effective teacher I can be for those kids. I don't want to just be there as the cancer man in his wheelchair who shows up at school. I want to bless them."

Our son spent an evening with the De Boers after Randy's surgery and reported, "They're so peaceful, Mom. Everything seems normal around there. Randy still cracks those puns."

I wasn't surprised. Pain and loving relationships have intersected often in Randy's life—and have trained him in the perseverance he needs to contend with his cancer. Here's how he tells the story:

> When I was twelve, my mom got breast cancer. She was sick for
> three years, sometimes better, sometimes worse. When I was fifteen,

she died, and I put up an emotional shield. It was so hard. She was such a giving person, not just to us but to others too. Always baking for people, taking groceries to families in the tenements. She showed us how to put others first. After she was gone, my dad was lonely but never once asked, "Why me?" He never complained about caring for us four kids alone. He was stable, steady, faithful, loving. He showed us how to go on and how to trust God.

Then in 1991 my sister Karla died in a rollover accident. That familiar pain hit us, but between my mom's and Karla's deaths, we began to realize, as my dad put it, that it's "good to bring things out in the open." I was beginning to learn not to hide my feelings but to be honest and open about them. I was starting to realize that by talking with my family, I could have someone help me process my pain.

Five years later my other sister, Rhonda, died of breast cancer—just like my mom had. No, it wasn't any easier this time, but we knew we'd get through it. This time our families talked openly about our emotions throughout her illness and about the future and the past. I wish we had been as openly supportive when Mom was sick—but we didn't know how. Now we do.

My dad told me, "Trust; trust; trust. Hope; hope; hope. Pray; pray; pray. I always remember that. Strange as it may seem, all this grief has resulted in added security, love, and commitment—which has brought even more good than happened before all this pain. I'm honestly not shaken. And Jan [Randy's wife] has been a rock for the kids and me. Going through this with her has only deepened my faith in God. And the perseverance? Faith is everything to perseverance.

I thought about the generational impact of Randy's example when I told him about traits I saw in his son Matt in the classroom, when he visited with us at home, or went camping with us at the lake. "Matt has learned a lot already," I said. He's always encouraged our son to persevere—in his work and in his relationships with people and with God. Matt's a steady, loving kid who keeps his commitments. Watching you and Jan, I see where he learned it."

"Let us run with perseverance the race marked out for us," writes the apostle Paul in Hebrews 12. "One thing I do: Forgetting what is behind and straining toward what is ahead, I press on toward the . . . goal" (Philippians 3:13–14). Adversity (no matter how great) in tandem with at least one trusted, steadfast adult (who can lead the young person through it) develops that child's perseverance—a sturdy timber in the structure of success.

Remember . . .

- Perseverance empowers us to endure adversity and sustain hope.
- Adversity interpreted by a caring adult can help a child develop perseverance—a precursor to maturity, completeness, and success.
- Faith is everything to perseverance.

Chapter Seven

Responsibility for Our Actions

> One of the annoying things about believing in free
> will and individual responsibility is the difficulty of
> finding somebody to blame your problems on. And
> when you do find somebody, it's remarkable how
> often his picture turns up on your driver's license.
> —P. J. O'Rourke

When I [Tim] was seven years old, I dared my five-year-old brother to jump out of the upstairs window onto the driveway. He promptly clambered onto the window ledge, leaped off, and crumpled in a heap on the pavement below!

Though not all big brothers are so reckless, children do experiment constantly. A sister, trying to influence her sibling, can show kindness to him one moment and punch him the next. A four-year-old can step on a goldfish just to see its guts squeeze out. Seven-year-olds can dare little brothers to hurl themselves out of windows.

While jumping out of a second-story window is dangerous, much of childhood experimentation is harmless, normal, and healthy. As I [Tim] found out, it's also an important ingredient in learning responsibility. When kids experience a reprimand, a dead fish, or a beloved little brother unconscious (he recovered fully), they encounter the valuable world of consequences.

How does this relate to the At-Promise paradigm? See if this sounds familiar: when we combine adversity's consequences with a trusted adult's guidance, we can teach children to own their actions. In fact, interpreted adversity forms the ideological bedrock for developing responsibility. Taking responsibility for one's own actions is a precursor to making the sorts of choices that can lead to success.

AT-PROMISE PRINCIPLE 4: Responsibility for our actions keeps us from blaming others and teaches us that our choices have impact.

Helpless People Blame Others and Give Up

In Chapter Six you read about learned helplessness and how it causes both kids and adults to quit.[1] Let's extend that concept one step farther: quitters tend to blame. When we feel helpless (a synonym for hopeless) to improve our situation, we tend to blame other people, our own emotional or intellectual inadequacies, timing, finances, physical limitations, geography, technology, weather, history, and so on. If you can think of it, someone's probably identified it as a cause of failure. People often place blame when they see no way out of a dilemma.

Too often we promote the belief that circumstances condemn children to making poor choices. We minimize or ignore their own power to choose, to contradict those negative predictions. Someone who sees Ronna as at risk would say she quit school because she comes from a single-parent, alcoholic home, or that Arturo deals drugs because of the kids with whom he hangs out. Of course, fifteen-year-old Marita is pregnant because her mother and grandmother also had babies at that age. Ask James, whose dad is in trouble with the law, why he got a speeding ticket. Well-schooled in at-risk victimization, he will tell you the thirty-five mile per hour speed limit along that country road is "way too slow. And besides, the cop has it out for me." Claire says she screamed abusively at her mother because her mom arrived late picking her up after the movie.

These illustrations suggest a grave lack of responsibility for one's actions among many young people. Kids too often toss responsible behavior out the window when impulses convince them to take a riskier course. Consider this example: large numbers of young people engage in sexual activity without weighing the ramifications. Though they have the choice to abstain from sex and to take adequate measures to guard against pregnancy or disease, many abdicate that responsibility. Later they blame their pregnancy or infection on their partner, on ignorance, or on their own inability to say no to sex. When we choose to place blame, and to see ourselves as helpless victims when we actually have empowering choices, we ignore our responsibility to act in a manner that doesn't harm or destroy.

When We Let Kids off the Hook, We Let Them Down

We regularly miss opportunities to teach children to take responsibility for their behaviors. Thousands of young people commit crimes while under the influence of drugs or alcohol. Violations range from driving under the influence to property damage to accidents to assault and murder. Too often courts end up letting those kids off the hook for the same kinds of reasons parents regularly let their children off the hook for less serious behaviors.

Whether infractions are serious or minor, we can neglect to give kids empowering discipline because we disregard the power of pain as a teacher. We believe that telling children what they did wrong and why they shouldn't do it again will be enough. We think that if we're just reasonable and loving enough, they'll listen and change their ways and won't need the discomfort of consequences. We don't want them to hurt, and we long to give them another chance, a fresh start. We may fear alienating them with discipline that costs them comfort.

Unfortunately, too often the lesson kids learn from leniency is that they can misbehave and nothing will happen. Many children will never understand the grace of a true fresh start until they grapple with consequences that build personal responsibility. Adversity's consequences are not antithetical to grace.

Second, many of us are already overloaded with problems. Whether we are exhausted parents and teachers, burdened social workers or probation officers, or administrators of crowded jails and court systems, we don't have the resources or energy to call those kids to account and then effectively stick with them through the consequences.

Therein lies the real problem. If we expect our kids to be responsible for their actions, then we must be responsible for ours too. That takes work and teamwork. After a child's infraction, our initial good intentions can quickly slide away as other pressures compete for our attention. When the biology teacher insists that Jolie, who is failing her last-hour class, stay fifteen minutes after school each day, the teacher intends both to discipline her for her irresponsibility and to help her catch up. The plan seems doable, until the teacher is summoned to a faculty meeting one day, a parent's phone call the next, and her own child's soccer game on yet another. Before long Jolie's after-school time with the teacher becomes just one more hit-and-miss experience in her life. What's worse, her teacher is modeling the inconsistency that got Jolie in trouble in the first place. *Why should I care?* Jolie thinks. *My parents don't.* (She assumes this because of their many distractions.) *My teachers don't either.*

After sixteen-year-old Rick got his second traffic ticket, his parents pulled his driving privileges for a month. That meant that Rick, who lived several miles out of town, needed rides from family members to get to and from basketball practice. "This stinks," his older brother complained, after hauling Rick back and forth several times. "Rick got the tickets, but I feel like I'm getting punished." His parents nodded wearily. A week after they took his license away, Rick had it back. The cost of disciplining him kept them from following through. By the end of the month, Rick had his third ticket.

Empowered Kids Take Responsibility

The At-Promise perspective claims that neither we nor the children we mentor are helpless over temptations to engage in risky behavior, regardless of how deeply entrenched that behavior is in our families. The apostle Paul gives the biblical view of that truth:

"No temptation has seized you except what is common to man. And God is faithful; he will not let you be tempted beyond what you can bear. But when you are tempted, he will also provide a way out so that you can stand up under it" (1 Corinthians 10:13). God's truth backs us up when we tell young people that they can resist temptation. They can take responsibility and choose wisely before destructive behavior occurs. Circumstances and people can disappoint us. But as At-Promise adults, we can teach our At-Promise children that no matter how difficult their lives or how debilitating their adversity (or ease), they can choose how to respond. We can teach them that their success depends upon those choices.

Do At-Promise folks (or any others) claim God's escape route and choose well every time? Of course not. Every person is sinful. But when we do make mistakes, claiming helplessness is not the answer. Then, and especially then, we are still responsible for our actions. The sooner we acknowledge our errors, our poor choices, the sooner we can shift our courses. We can own the wrongs, make redemptive decisions in response to them, and begin again to succeed.

Taking responsibility for our actions is the first step to healing and forgiveness. When we stop trying to cover our mistakes by blaming, we open our innermost parts to God's transforming work. When we fess up and admit, "I did it," or "that's my problem, and I am truly sorry," we begin to bring change and success into the midst of the mess.

Promise Fulfilled Through Responsibility

Dr. Tommy Lewis, who grew up on the Navajo reservation, is the former president of Northwest Indian College. I [Tim] was serving as associate director of the education department at that institution when I met him. Tommy readily took responsibility for the college's functioning, even when—from my perspective—some circumstances were completely beyond his control. I admired his honorable behavior and knew I could learn much from this man.

Whenever I could, I stopped by his office, where he often illustrated his wisdom with stories about growing up on the reservation.

I quickly realized that a powerful adult in Tommy's life had shown him how to weave an At-Promise thread through each of his life stories, stories that inevitably culminated at his mother's house. Integrity, strength, and honor resided in Tommy's mom. She had little formal education, but she held a Ph.D. when it came to living wisely within her Native American tradition. Forty years later her son recalled her words:

> Many people don't think about breathing. They take air for granted, think they will always suck it in and live a minute longer. But from our traditional teachings, we know that breath is sacred. It can be taken away in a second.
>
> Life is short; Dad and I are not going to be here for the rest of your life, Tommy. One of these days, we are going to flame out. When that happens, you are going to have to be strong. You are going to have to go on and carry your responsibilities. So while you have the time, don't be lazy. Don't make excuses. Don't blame other people for your problems. You will have to suffer. Getting from here to there in life is tough. Life is tough. Not everything is going to be perfect, but it is up to you to make the most of it.

Tommy learned much about responsibility from his mother, and he models her wisdom. I grew from his mentorship.

As a member of the Saponny tribe, I [Tim] understand that for Native American children, significant trials and pain are not difficult to come by. Native Americans are victims of violence more often than any other ethnic group in the United States.[2] By any standard, this is a heartbreaking fact. This adversity causes immense pain and harm.

A second, more far-reaching and long-lived devastation happens when suffering young people choose to remain victimized by adversity (a choice Tommy rejected). The hopelessness of helplessness, though it is something we learn and choose, incapacitates its sufferers as surely as if they truly were helpless, which they are not. This second problem saturates the lives of many of our children.

Responsibility Requires an Inner Locus of Control

A groundswell of educators and developmental psychologists understands that the willingness to take responsibility for one's actions is one of the most important attributes a child can possess. Bernard Wiener's attributional theory suggests that children can shed the victim mentality that contributes to learned helplessness. They can stop blaming and can instead take responsibility for their lives, like Dr. Tommy Lewis has. They can develop the skill of recognizing multiple options for action even when bad things beyond their control happen to them.[3]

How well people learn that skill can be determined by their "locus of control." According to researcher Julian Rotter, who coined the term, people can think they have a lot of control over their own lives, or they can think they have very little. Those perceptions fall along a continuum between two extremes, between an inner locus of control or an outer one. People with a mostly external locus of control assign their successes and failures to fate, luck, and situations they cannot affect or control. They usually feel powerless to change themselves or their circumstances.[4]

Conversely, those of us who have developed a mostly internal locus of control believe that success and failure are up to us. We trust that reinforcements (positive consequences) result from hard work and planning, which enable us to control outcomes. An inner locus of control is associated with high tolerance of stress;[5] so even when facing enormous challenges, we believe we can take steps to make things happen, and we do. This attitude not only enables us to dodge helplessness and victimization and to assume responsibility for our actions but also facilitates the character trait of perseverance we described in Chapter Six. When we and our kids have this belief, we are motivated to modify our attitudes and behavior so that we can change our risk-laden environment and expedite success.

Internal Locus of Control for Christians

Christian thinking adds another dimension to the locus-of-control concept. Rather than seeing ourselves as the captains of our destiny, believers acknowledge the all-knowing, all-powerful Lord. When we depend upon Him, He makes available the self-discipline to choose wisely (though each one of us certainly has the option to make poor choices if he or she wants to). Though we may not have the capability to control events or people besides ourselves, we can be in control, freely making choices within the framework of circumstances God has allowed us. When we make choices from under that umbrella of freedom, we know the choices are ours; we can take responsibility for our actions.

How Do We Teach Responsibility?

Clearly, taking responsibility is an important lesson for children to learn. So how do we teach it? Where can we start?

Unless we hold them accountable for what they do, children will not assume full ownership of their actions. When we discipline our kids in a way that develops responsibility (because we love them), we naturally combine adversity and relationship, the At-Promise combination that can lead to success.

Oh, this is easy to prescribe but not so easy to carry out. We [Tim and Cheryl] speak from experience with our collective children, now ages five to twenty, when we say this is a cinch to write—but most difficult to do consistently and lovingly. As we said earlier, at one time or another many caregivers find it more convenient to let issues slide when children need correction. Those of us who have tried to avoid necessary conflict with children may be inclined to sweep a child's negative behavior under the rug, when instead we should call attention to it and offer appropriate consequences. As we ignore their behavior, we may ask, *Aren't we called to love those kids unconditionally?*

Yes, we are. That's why we hold children accountable. Disciplining the young people in our care, children with whom we have built relationships, is one of the most loving acts we can do for them. How much better for them to learn responsibility early on (and alongside adults who care about them) than later, when stakes may be higher and others involved may be indifferent or hostile. When we discipline kids wisely, we are offering them love like that which God offers us. Proverbs 3:12 explains: "the Lord disciplines those he loves, as a father the son he delights in."

Discipline helps young people understand the consequences of foolish actions and tells the child that he or she alone is responsible for that outcome. What a gift! When discipline is repeated and consistent in the context of a well-maintained, love-based relationship, even a recalcitrant child can learn to take responsibility for his or her actions. Once the child's conscience—rather than parents, teachers, or law enforcement officers—begins to direct that ownership, the child has strengthened her inner locus of control.

Practically speaking, the discipline that develops responsibility takes many forms, which depend on the adult's role in the child's life; the child's age; the child's and adult's temperaments, traditions, and histories. We may remove privileges, require financial compensation or public apology, issue time-outs, or apply any of a myriad of other disciplinary measures. Sometimes we simply need to step out of the way and allow natural consequences.

Whatever the means of discipline, we must commit to it. If Jake and Andre wrestle in the living room (against house rules) and break the fish tank, we can have them clean up the mess and then pay to replace the tank and the fish. If eighth-grade Beth lies to a teacher about her whereabouts, that teacher can respond by restricting her freedom until she earns the teacher's trust back. If Jennifer overspends early in the month, her parents can refuse to bail her out by giving or loaning her money. The pain that her mismanagement causes can bless her future financial decision making, if we don't interfere. Disciplining kids in any of these scenarios will cost us time and energy, but we mustn't abandon our efforts.

We Can Expect Conflict

What if we stand our ground and our kids resist all the more? What if we have tried to build trusting relationships with our children and have given them consequences (adversity) for their foolish choices, but they resist us at every turn? We're feeling punished, and they're refusing to take responsibility for their actions. In fact, they're blaming us for their problems!

Well, we can expect conflict. Remember, if they're experiencing adversity, as we walk though it with them, we will too. But we've lived longer and hopefully know how to wait it out even when it's uncomfortable and even when, by all appearances, we think our child will never learn. Educational and psychological research has tested and God has affirmed this: interpreted adversity really can bless our children. Eugene Peterson, in his paraphrase of Hebrews 12, writes, "God is educating you; that's why you must never drop out. He's treating you as dear children. This trouble you're in isn't punishment; it's *training*, the normal experience of children. Only irresponsible parents leave children to fend for themselves. Would you prefer an irresponsible God?"[6]

We Can Hope

Discipline, like all of adversity's training, can help our children succeed by motivating them to take responsibility for their actions. When our kids have to own their choices, they learn responsibility, another essential piece of At-Promise character.

Remember . . .

- Responsibility for our actions keeps us from blaming others and teaches us that our choices have impact.

- When we choose to place blame, and to see ourselves as help-less victims when we actually have empowering choices, we ignore our responsibility to act in a manner that doesn't harm or destroy.
- Adversity's consequences are not antithetical to grace.
- The hopelessness of helplessness, though it is something we learn and choose, incapacitates its sufferers as surely as if they truly were helpless, which they are not.

Chapter Eight

Optimism

You're never stuck. You always have options.

—*Mom Stuart*

Every once in a while, you meet someone whose perspective on the world challenges you at the deepest level. In my case [Tim's], I married that someone's daughter. When I first met my father-in-law, Jim Janz, he was like no one I had ever met before; his sheer optimism about people made me suspicious, and yet his positive outlook was contagious. Not only did this successful businessman have genuine hope for people, he spent his days speaking that hope into their lives. Children, waiters, bank tellers, car dealers, business executives, university presidents, and politicians seemed to hold their heads a little higher after Jim had been around. His daily interactions with people came as refreshing air in a stifling, pessimistic world.

Whenever I was with him, I watched people seek Jim's presence. Almost daily and in places ranging from airport check-in lines to church lobbies to restaurants, people grabbed a moment with him to express the positive impact he made on their lives (and to let in a little more sunshine).

The more time I spent with my father-in-law after I married Mona, the more I began to ask myself: *What would happen to my students if I saw them in the same optimistic way that Jim saw business associates and hotel valets? If my eyes were trained to focus on the promise of children instead of on their shortcomings, what difference would that make? And what if parents and educators around the globe would begin to speak authentic optimism and hope into every child's life, so that they held their heads a little higher every day? If this could happen, I thought, we could truly change the world.*

Of course, many students spend their days rotating through classrooms and shuffling through the hallway crowds, hoping to meet a teacher like Jim Janz. Many teachers, as well, stare out into a sea of student faces, looking for those who've tasted true optimism. Unfortunately, sometimes a teacher lands on the opposite: a portrait of pessimism that can't be erased from her memory even after intervening decades.

Though hundreds of students moved through my classrooms over the years, I [Cheryl] don't remember any girl crabbier than one I met during my second year of teaching. Nyssa still stands out as the most negative, critical teenager I have ever encountered. Her attitude smelled like roadkill in August.

She found fault with everything and everyone, including and especially herself. Peers and teachers had tried, but no one could convince her to see anything positive. She directed her energies to fattening up her complaints. She fried up every nitpicky little thing she could find and tossed it to her grumblings. Her bad attitude gobbled up those nasty morsels and grew more and more vocal.

I won't trouble you with the unpleasant details. You know what happened. She was miserable and miserable to be around, and her inclination to contribute anything positive to anyone was nil. Her grousing ruined her relationships and her days. She rebuffed our efforts to reach out to her, so most of us teachers kept our distance and just endured her. One year later my husband and I moved across the state, and I lost track of her.

To this day I am haunted by the fact that we gave up on Nyssa, and I pray that someone somewhere stuck with her long enough to build trust with her—and to teach her that optimism is a choice. Nyssa, I suspect, did what many of us do, whether we are young or old: she let her feelings and faulty perceptions dictate how she would choose to think rather than choosing true, positive thoughts that could shape her feelings. For reasons none of us were privy to, Nyssa felt that her teachers, her peers, and she herself were intolerable, miserable, and hopeless; and she acted as if those feelings were unchangeable.

In the years since, I have learned that no matter what had happened to make Nyssa so unhappy, her attitude was something she still had control over, even if she couldn't change one other thing about her life. Only she didn't know that. She needed someone to love her enough to show her that though adversity is a fact of life, her bitterness and misery didn't have to be. If she had decided to listen, someone could have redirected her away from believing what her feelings and faulty thoughts told her and then could have shown her how to capture her thoughts and point them toward something better.

Clearly, that optimism can encourage our children. They watch and listen to how we interpret our world. If we want our kids to be optimistic, then we must choose an optimistic attitude about their futures, especially when they have not yet developed it themselves. We teachers failed to do that for Nyssa when we quit trying to connect with her.

Adversity (pain, challenges, trials, afflictions, hurts, harms, disappointments, failures) experienced without interpretation is the number one contributor to pessimism in our children. If we had shown hope for Nyssa, perhaps we could have taught her specific, authentic ways to combat that pessimism and to develop optimism by taking her own thoughts captive. This chapter describes how.

AT-PROMISE PRINCIPLE 5: Optimism gives us lenses of hope through which we can see positive possibilities in the midst of pain.

How Can You Say That?

A couple of years ago, I [Cheryl] stood in the parking lot at the high school, talking to Tara, a student who, at the tender age of seventeen, was tired of hurting because of a dad who had left the family without saying good-bye, a depressed mom, friends who wouldn't stand by her, an overweight body that boys had teased her about, and a mind that hopped and jumped and wouldn't concentrate. She had been trying some painkillers: she'd had sex twice (with two different boys), and she had started to smoke and drink. She said that though her heart raced with anxiety, she almost felt better—because the temporary pleasures took her mind away from all that hurt.

I cried with her and hugged her. Then I told her how precious she was, how much promise she had, and how I loved her. "Thanks, Mrs. B.," she said. "But so what? Your caring about me doesn't really change anything. No offense or anything, but just because you say it doesn't mean it's true. People say stuff all the time, but people change their minds once they get to know me. They never stick around."

She continued: "I'm dumb in school. I'm fat and ugly. Boys think I'm useful for only one thing. How can I be precious? What do I have to hope for?"

Let's look at the heart of Tara's questions. Wasn't she asking why she was valuable? Why she was worth loving? Why she should be optimistic? Tara needed more than a self-esteem message teaching her to mouth words of self-affirmation. She needed more than the opinions of potentially fickle people cheerleading her into a superficially bright attitude. To her, such words were empty, groundless flattery that changed nothing. In her mind to pretend they were true would be fraudulent, another temporary fix. Tara wanted me to show her why they were true, why she should even try to kindle optimism. And my reason needed to be grounded, substantial. Its truth needed to stand firm when adversity threatened to crush her future hopes.

The Self-Esteem Movement Has Failed

Hers are critical questions. For the last thirty years, the self-esteem movement has tried to convince children like Tara that they are indeed valuable, capable, and worthy of esteem. People have spent hundreds of thousands—no, millions—of hours and dollars attempting to convey that message to young people. The culture has adopted a goal of feeling good about yourself that proponents plaster on magazine and textbook pages, TV screens, and airwaves. Their intentions are legitimate, but they have failed miserably. According to Dr. Martin Seligman, author of *The Optimistic Child*, kids today are more depressed and pessimistic than at any time in history![1] Why are kids so pessimistic? Maybe kids look on the dark side because they have lost hope for their future.

Why? Because, as Tara said, simply telling kids they're wonderful doesn't make it so. They want proof, and that proof doesn't lie in groundless words, the affirmation of which those kids are supposed to drum up from somewhere inside their hurting, confused insides.

The self-esteem movement has failed to promote an optimistic outlook and resulting success in children because most advocates have attempted to create self-worth out of a void. They identify this ungrounded self-esteem as the point of origin for identity and success. "Kids should value themselves," proponents say, "because they're valuable. They're valuable because we value them . . . because they're valuable." The circular argument chases its tail and goes nowhere.

In a distorted form of unconditional acceptance, educators inflate grades, minimize failures, reduce accountability for actions, and provide empty praise; somehow thinking that setting lower expectations for children to measure up to will make them feel more successful. But kids don't believe that flattery, and they don't respect low standards. Affirmations coming from that setting are simply too flimsy to be a foundation for successful identity and achievement. Meanwhile, the more kids try to make sense of it all, the more hopeless and helpless they become, and their articulated self-worth actually drops. They can't make a faulty premise work, no matter how hard they try.

Why Be Optimistic? How?

So how do we answer Tara's questions? How can we show her and other children that they are valuable, that they are worth loving, that they have promise and can succeed in life—in short, that they can view the future with optimism?

First, we can quit trying to convince them to have high self-esteem. Telling them to like and value themselves is like sending them to the garden to pick the peas—only the peas have never been planted, much less watered, fertilized, and cultivated. Cheering for the withered peas sealed in the garden store's package doesn't raise the crop. Just as delicious peas are the result of sowing and care, appropriate self-esteem is a by-product of choices and behavior—not the other way around.

We answer kids' questions about their self-worth by providing them with knowledge and tools to cultivate their optimism. We want a twofold optimism for them: one founded on both love-based identity and on realistic self-efficacy.

Why will optimism help young people hope? Because when they are optimistic, they are realizing that true success is within their grasp. By *success*, we don't mean being thin, rich, intelligent, talented, famous, gifted, or athletic. Although those traits may play a role in some individuals' success, they neither guarantee success nor are they necessary for it. (What a relief!) Instead, young people are absolutely capable of succeeding because true success, the sort with lasting significance, means making a positive contribution to the moral and social fabric of society. A person who knows she can succeed regardless of her circumstances can approach life optimistically.

How can we help children optimistically anticipate success? Three ways:

- We give them opportunities and encouragement to achieve mastery, which produces self-efficacy or a can-do attitude.
- We show them their true identity based on God's promises.
- We show them that all difficulties contribute to growth; trials are part of the success equation.

In other words, we give them hope, a reason to be optimistic. When they—and we who have come alongside them—direct energy into developing and using their gifts, skills, and talents, their confidence that they can conquer other challenges will rise. When we give them the truth about themselves from God's timeless, loving perspective and—not merely the opinions of well-meaning but inconsistent people, they can ground their self-evaluation on rock-solid unchangeable fact. When we show them how to use the often hidden benefits of pain and trials, their character will grow. As we do, we are teaching them to capture their thoughts and develop hope: the seed of optimism, a key crop in success's garden.

Mastery and Self-Efficacy

In earlier chapters we substantiated the value of adversity. Children need experiences that evoke frustration, failure, disappointment, anger, and worry. Unless a child crashes into those difficulties, he will never learn how to overcome them. As we all know, those painful feelings can prompt him to do one of two things: he can quit, or he can try again and again. The number of his attempts depends on the degree of his discomfort, his determination, and the support of a caring mentor who encourages the child to keep working at it. When the child at last succeeds after all those attempts, he has achieved mastery.

When the child repeats a pattern of pain, perseverance, and success in other situations, the child learns to recognize the pattern and to believe that he can follow it in order to reach other difficult goals. He transfers the experience of mastery into a belief in self-efficacy, which facilitates adaptation, coping, and achievement.[2] Research shows that kids with self-efficacy achieve more in school.[3]

Most of us who work with children have seen the contrast between those without self-efficacy and those with it. Some children won't attempt any organized activity, especially anything new. When encouraged to participate, they answer with, "I can't." And they believe it! Mired in learned helplessness, they won't try unfamiliar games, exercises, or projects. Mastery has eluded them, as has self-efficacy.

Other children, however, will try any activity, even if they have never done it before. When they persevere like this, and when they succeed because they persevered, they learn to believe that they can succeed in other areas as well. Self-efficacy results. They begin to comprehend the power of a can-do attitude. As a result, they become even more optimistic, more hopeful. Those who repeatedly master tasks enjoy that optimism.

Granted, self-efficacy is conditional. That means it is hooked to performance and accomplishment, the flip side of which is failure. But when children learn the role a tested optimistic attitude plays in multiplying accomplishment and overcoming defeats, they will feel more capable and willing to face challenges, more convinced they can do it!

Psychologist Martin Seligman has identified three questions whose answers predict whether a child will approach trials helplessly or optimistically. He calls it the child's "explanatory style," how she explains causes of life events. He writes, "When a child does badly, she asks herself 'Why?' There are always three aspects to the answer she comes up with: *who* is to blame, *how long* will it last, and *how much of her life* will be undermined. . . . Feeling bad about the self does not directly cause failure. The belief that problems will last forever and undermine everything, in contrast, directly causes your child to stop trying. Giving up leads to more failure, which then goes on to undermine feelings of self-esteem."[4]

But when a young person takes responsibility for his mistakes, whether they be 1 percent or 100 percent of a problem, he is empowered. His personal actions make a difference! When that child believes that he can change or eliminate his adversity, he can begin to formulate a plan of action to do so. And when the student believes that his adversity is localized, only existing within confined parameters of life, he can cope with the difficulty rather than be overwhelmed by it.[5] Children who learn that they can choose responses to adversity can approach trials with self-efficacy. They can optimistically resolve trials. In fact, when they see adversity as a necessary part of growth's equation, then adversity itself is no longer a cause for pessimism but can instead contribute to optimistic thinking!

Identity Based on God's Promises

Optimism that develops because of self-efficacy's can-do attitude is conditional or earned optimism. Performance and mastery determine the degree of earned optimism a child will apply to new situations. Although conditional optimism certainly helps people contribute positively to society's moral and social warp and woof, optimism that is a by-product of human mastery is more vulnerable to injury. When a diving accident steals a young person's mastery by making her a quadriplegic or when mental disability prevents any mastery at all, what then? How can children be optimistic when skill or capabilities lessen or never develop in the first place?

Because conditional optimism can fail, children also need the optimism that grows from God-given identity. A child can't earn this optimism; it is unconditional. That means he or she can never lose it! It arises from a permanent identity.

This identity is a free gift. Unlike the flighty assessments of people who extend and retract the scepter of fame or popularity or applause or esteem at a whim, God-given identity can't be returned, exchanged, or altered. From birth it extends into every cell of our bodies and into our very souls (Genesis 5:1–2; Psalm 139).

Capturing Thoughts

Tara, Nyssa, and every child can choose an optimistic attitude when they trust their intrinsic identities as God's image bearers. When that happens, they will feel safe and loved enough to look honestly at their roles in problems—rather than defensively denying their part or, conversely, blaming themselves for too much of the difficulty. As a result, they can make changes for the better in their choices and behavior. They learn to mitigate the negative effects of their pain and can even recognize pain's usefulness. They learn that even in the most serious situation, God will keep their souls intact. The Lord, who loves them, wields enough power to redeem even the worst stuff. Everything will eventually be OK.

The result of this kind of thinking? Enhanced hope that translates into optimistic attitudes and optimistic living. God explains: "We take captive every thought to make it obedient to Christ" (2 Corinthians 10:5). We don't just let our thoughts tag along after our fickle, tyrannical feelings. Once we've lassoed those thoughts, here's what we do with them: we concentrate on "whatever is true, whatever is noble, whatever is right, whatever is pure, whatever is lovely, whatever is admirable—if anything is excellent or praiseworthy . . . [we] think about such things" (Philippians 4:8).

A hopeful, optimistic person can more easily choose to contribute positively, morally, and socially to society than can a depressed, pessimistic one. And when she does, she succeeds.

Remember . . .

- Though adversity is a fact of life, bitterness and misery don't have to be.

- If we want our kids to be optimistic, then we must choose an optimistic attitude about their futures—especially when they have not yet developed it themselves.

- The self-esteem movement has failed to promote an optimistic outlook and resulting success in children because most advocates have attempted to create self-worth out of a void.

- We want a twofold optimism for them: one founded on both love-based identity and realistic self-efficacy.

- When we see adversity as a necessary part of growth's equation, then adversity itself is no longer a cause for pessimism but can instead contribute to optimistic thinking!

Chapter Nine

Motivation from Identity

Nothing hinders faith more than the failure to
appreciate who you are.

—*Colin Urquhart*

While in his twenties, Jean Valjean, out of work and desperate to provide for his widowed sister and her seven children, breaks a bakery window with his fist and steals a loaf of bread. That act sends Valjean to prison, where he spends the next nineteen years of his life. Author Victor Hugo, describing Valjean in his classic novel *Les Misérables*, reports that Valjean enters prison as a sensitive tree-pruner, tearful about his sentence and concerned about the children in his care; but he emerges from his incarceration as a tough, impassive man, a hardened criminal.

The newly paroled Valjean, starving and repeatedly rejected, encounters the kindly bishop of Digne, who welcomes Valjean into his home for a hearty meal and a clean bed. Valjean cannot comprehend the bishop's kindness. "I am a convict!" Valjean exclaims to the old man.

"I know who you are," the bishop replies as he continues to treat Valjean with respect and honor, calling Valjean "brother" and "friend." The bishop's regard baffles Valjean, who does not know how to respond. He mumbles a thank-you and falls into bed.

In the middle of the night, Valjean awakens. Even as the prison tattoo under the skin of his forearm tells Valjean's history, prison's years of cruelty and hatred have tattooed Valjean with his criminal identity. Despite the bishop's hospitality, Valjean acts on that convict identity: he assaults the old man, then steals his silver and flees.

The next morning officers arrive at the bishop's door—with Valjean in tow. Caught with the goods, Valjean has told them that the silver is a gift from the bishop! The disbelieving gendarmes have returned to have the bishop identify the silver before they haul the suspect off to jail.

Then the bishop, who has seen Valjean's promise—his God-given identity—all along, does a most unexpected thing: he welcomes Valjean back as a friend and corroborates his story! Then he reenters the house, returns with two silver candlesticks, and gently chastens Valjean for forgetting them!

The bishop's gift of grace wrapped around that silver astounds Valjean and changes him forever. "Don't forget . . . Jean Valjean, my brother," the bishop says. "You no longer belong to evil. With this silver I've bought your soul. I've ransomed you from fear and hatred, and now I give you back to God."

Valjean is transformed into a successful man. He changes his name, builds a factory, and becomes the benevolent, wise mayor in his town. When one of his employees, Fantine, is dismissed for having an illegitimate child, she resorts to prostitution to pay for medication for her daughter, Cosette. Life on the streets takes its toll; brutality and disease debilitate Fantine. Valjean discovers her condition and takes her in, offering her food, care, and dignity.

Fantine's response to Valjean's mercy mimics that of Valjean when he sat at the bishop's table. She cries, "You don't understand! I'm a whore . . . and Cosette has no father!"

But Valjean sees more: he sees her promise and extends that identity to both Fantine and her daughter. "She [Cosette] has the Lord," he replies. "He is her Father, and you're his creation." When Fantine dies, having made her peace with God, Valjean, himself a child of God, raises Cosette with that same wonderful identity.[1]

AT-PROMISE PRINCIPLE 6: Motivation from identity inspires us to live as individuals created in God's image, not as people labeled by our assets or deficits.

A person's identity motivates thoughts—and motivates the words and actions that spring from those beliefs about who we are. Like Jean Valjean, many young people have been handed mistaken identities—or have attached those flawed self-perceptions to themselves. Where do those internalized labels come from? Usually, people and events impose them on children over time, though even a single ugly, painful, or criminal event or a single interaction with a person can inject that faulty judgment into a child's understanding.

Once that happens, the child no longer sees the event as temporary and attached to an isolated set of circumstances but instead attaches the stigma to himself. The more he repeats the behavior, the more ingrained the label becomes. Over time he effectively cements those beliefs about himself into a solid identity.

Valjean, for instance, was a desperate young man who stole bread. Yes, the thievery was wrong, but the act did not make him a thief in his soul. Instead, nineteen brutal prison years, a permanent tattoo, and a police inspector (who refused to let his past die) labeled him a thief and convinced Valjean that the label was truly his identity. Because he believed it, he lived it out and stole the bishop's silver the first chance he got.

Our schools and streets and homes are packed with kids like these. At-risk eyesight sees Tom the alcoholic, Lucinda the tramp, Maria the cheater, Harris the druggie, Tamara the glutton. All are identities linked to children's behavior. Then, because kids believe the labels, they perpetuate and reinforce them, and so do adults and peers who watch the kids.

Whoa. Wait right there, you're thinking. *Haven't they brought those labels on themselves? They do that stuff again and again!* Yes, sometimes they do. But when we expect them to repeat their behaviors and label them accordingly, we only nail those negative identities into place a little more firmly.

Intrinsic Motivation Is Key to Success

According to the esteemed French philosopher Jean-Jacques Rousseau, the biggest challenge of education is the question of motivation. He believed that when children are self-motivated, the teacher cannot keep them from learning.[2] Most education research would support Rousseau's belief. In fact, the American Psychological Association has identified "intrinsic motivation" as one of twelve important learning principles.[3] The idea is that children learn more successfully when their own interest and natural curiosity motivates them.

Although we agree that intrinsic motivation is essential to a child's learning and development process, we also know that a child's interests and curiosity are temperamental. Our children's unlimited curiosity and ever-changing interests are some of the most wonderful and exciting characteristics of childhood; however, they should not form the basis of their motivation. Interests and desires are fickle and unpredictable.

Instead, children can be motivated to act out of their At-Promise identity, which states that they are uniquely and wonderfully made in the likeness of God. That identity is also intrinsic but doesn't waver with mood, circumstances, or fluctuating desires. It is steady, stable, and fabulous—as the following story illustrates.

Molly's adoptive parents, Dave and Anne Anderson, found Molly at an orphanage in Taiwan when she was four months old. Born in the 1980s to a mom who had probably taken the drug Thalidomide, Molly had flippers instead of arms, and her legs were different lengths. Her birth mother had discarded her, a fact that could have shaped her identity had Dave and Anne not brought her home to Washington State when she was seven months old.

But love transforms. Along with her new language, Molly learned her true identity, not as a discard but as a child created by God. When she joined her family on a mission trip to Mexico fourteen years later, her identity shaped her choices.

Her family was part of a group constructing a water system in a remote mountain settlement. Molly chipped in alongside the rest of the workers, applying glue to pipe fittings with a paintbrush she held between her toes. She tightened pipe joints by leaning into the sections and shoving hard with her shoulders. She wielded a shovel by perching the handle atop one shoulder, stabilizing it under her chin, and then gripping it with her other shoulder and armpit.

Despite her hard work, the villagers ignored her. Though they mingled freely with the rest of the team, Molly's disabilities alienated them. Villagers turned their backs to her, treated her as if she were invisible. In her hometown Molly had grown accustomed to stares when people first saw her but had never seen others act so afraid and uncomfortable around her. She told me [Cheryl] how she struggled with their rejection and how she wondered if she should have come on the trip at all.

The impasse, she said, led her to pray this: *Lord, You say that You created me and that I am fearfully and wonderfully made. I believe you and trust that you made me this way for a purpose. My disability wasn't a mistake. These people don't know that, though. How can I reach out to them if they won't even come near me?*

The day after that prayer began like the others: she worked long hours alone. But midday a group of children from the school arrived at the construction site, wanting to meet Molly, whom they had heard about from the villagers who watched her from a distance. Eventually, the adults followed, and by the time the project was finished, her impact was clear. Molly's faithful work and her loving interaction had demonstrated God's value of every person more than anything the other team members said or did. A local woman disabled by polio even began to see that her twisted body didn't have to be a curse but could instead be used for good!

Molly's joyful, industrious response to adversity infused a number of villagers with hope and introduced them to God's unconditional love and purpose for every one of them. Without a doubt her identity helped her contribute positively to their community.

(And you should see that girl play badminton!)

An Identity Based on Deficiencies

Identifying oneself by deficiencies has become popular these days. Begun as an attempt to be more transparent and honest, self-deprecation has become a badge of honor for many and an excuse for failure for some. When we identify ourselves and our children as alcoholics, addicts, anorexics, or any of countless other labels, we are branding negatives onto ourselves and our kids, as if those descriptions will last a lifetime. When we label children as being depressive, having attention deficit disorder, being at risk, or using various other negative terms, we suggest to them that the label is part of a permanent identity. Negative labeling can trap our children by dictating and even predicting their behavior.

Conditional Versus Unconditional Identity

Instead, let's do the opposite! Because we can affect young people's identities, let's help them extract and expel the identities that limit and destroy them. Their capabilities, their connection with people, and their distinctiveness as children of God can give them glimpses of who they are. Let's help them discover life-giving identity that will motivate them toward success!

In Chapter Eight we talked about mastery's contribution to optimism. Helping children master tasks is also a way of helping them to create a healthy identity. Every time a child learns more about math, reading, animal care, tennis, first aid, or piano, he is developing self-efficacy, the can-do attitude that flows from having accomplished something. Can-do thinking convinces a child that he can do other new things as well. The confidence that comes from self-efficacy is valuable and pivotal to success. We are wise to foster it. But let's not confuse a can-do attitude that comes from conditional self-efficacy with the deep confidence that comes from an unconditional identity. Above and beyond task mastery and the motivation it sparks, kids need a deep sense of identity to ground them, to send down roots that will keep them standing in the fiercest storms.

How can we instill that certainty in them so that their motivation becomes truly intrinsic? For adults to believe in children's identity is one thing; for children to believe in their own God-given identity and to have their actions motivated by that identity is another. How can we help kids understand their identity the way

Maggie, my [Cheryl's] daughter's friend and teammate, does? During the high school volleyball season, I watched Maggie's lips move every time she served the ball. When I later asked her what she was saying, she smiled and said, "I was telling myself, 'I can do all things through Christ, who strengthens me.'" As her former teacher, I have seen her carry that certainty into her schoolwork and her relationships.

Tell Children Who They Are

First, we regularly tell children who they are. One way or another, we convey to kids that they are beloved, precious children of God. They have purpose. He has made them to have his traits; He will always love them and help them; and He will carry them through even the roughest of times.

Amy Kane grew up in a single-parent family. Though she loved and cared for her children to the best of her ability, Amy's mom carried deep sadness and loneliness, as well as physical pain, that caused her to withdraw from those who could have supported her. At times she would try to numb her pain with alcohol and prescription drugs, but her behavior only drove her deeper into her isolation. Consequently, her sons, Amy's brothers, rebelled, wanting a life different than that in their conflict-filled home. The whole scenario could have been a ticket to disaster for Amy.

When I [Tim] asked Amy what happened in her life that gave her a fighting chance, she told me about a family that discreetly and respectfully gave her a sense of belonging.

> I met my best girlfriend, Sonja, in the third grade. She lived around the corner from me, and her family knew what was going on in my home. They never could get close to my mom. I know Sonja's mom tried, but it was impossible. Though my mom could reach out to mentally or physically impaired people who needed a champion, she would not allow herself to be vulnerable or to show her own neediness. She used an aloof iciness to protect herself from further

hurt; she would cut off anyone who approached her with kindness or who offered her any help.

And so Sonja's family quietly included me. I knew I was loved like a daughter. . . . I think they really took me in that way. Sonja's dad had red hair, and I had red hair—but no one else in their family did. When I went swimming with them, people would figure that I was the daughter and Sonja was the visitor! We were that close.

Sonja's mom was our Brownie leader and our Girl Scout leader. We loved her and proclaimed that we would stay together forever. For years after the Girl Scout troop officially disbanded, after we were grown, we had reunions! Only one person had a divorce out of that troop. Amazing. A group of about fifteen of us and only one divorce! So the power of that group was huge. And Sonja's mom was wonderful. She loved me dearly. It pained her, I know, to see my pain. But her love was tremendous for me. . . . I have often thought that this family . . . saved me from going all those other directions.

The little things can often seal a child's At-Promise identity. Relational trivia that adults often overlook can initiate life-changing experiences for a child. For Amy even trips to the swimming pool and a head of red hair were influential.

These simple influences are much like a royal seal placed on a scroll. Though the seal is made only of wax, the king's power and authority represented by the imprint of his signet ring make it binding. Likewise, in our relationships with kids, we seal the At-Promise identity with a million goofy and seemingly insignificant things. However, when we place our stamp of approval on the life of a child, the seal can last a lifetime.

And Amy? The love from Sonja's family has helped Amy see beyond her own mother's pain-induced behavior to her mom's hidden strengths, to the tenacity that helped her mother carry on despite being poorly equipped to raise a family alone.

Amy has acquired her mother's heart for the disenfranchised. Today Amy owns a successful counseling and consulting practice where she helps victims of sexual abuse, as well as those suffering other great pain, loss, and loneliness. The sealing of her At-Promise identity with love and approval, and her mother's gritty courage, have helped Amy make a significant impact in the lives of thousands of hurting people.

Identity Motivates Behavior

Next, we show them how their identity can influence their behavior. Often they can first understand that identity in the context of family. My [Tim's] boys sometimes resort to hitting their sister while trying to get their own ways. I have tried every strategy known to man (and some that I just made up) to stop their abuse of my precious princess. One day, out of desperation I told my sons, "You are Stuarts. Stuart men don't hit their sisters, they defend them." To my surprise that concept made sense to them! For the first time, I had given them a reason to act out of their identity. Although it hasn't stopped all the warfare in our household, it has established a clear standard of expectations and behavior based on their identity, an identity that is unchangeable and secure.

Children are likely to model a revered adult, both in behavior and in ideology. When kids first learn how to follow and imitate their parents, they are well on their way to learning to follow and imitate their heavenly Father, the Lord who made them.

What? you ask. *They follow an adult to learn how to follow God?* Often, yes. The responsibility makes me quake in my boots. Even though it's scary, that fact makes me take the next step of showing kids their identity: I model it by doing all I can to build and act out of my own, God-honoring promise character. Kids will be watching.

Then, as children grow older, we can get out of the way. Our ultimate authority in our children's lives will lessen, and as it does, we can encourage their accountability directly to God. When my [Cheryl's] children reached middle-school age, they headed out the door to school, turnout, camps, parties, or just time with friends more and more often. I regularly whispered to them as I hugged them good-bye, "Remember Whose you are."

No longer could I follow them everywhere. Days of closely monitoring their behavior were past. Sure, their dad and I kept close tabs on them, as well as veto power over their decisions, but as their cognitive and moral reasoning matured, we made more room for their developing intrinsic motivation rather than having extrinsic parental rewards and discipline be their primary motivators. We encouraged them to act out of loving respect for the God who made them, as well as self-respect because of their identity as kids of the Creator and not just because of our praise or consequences.

Have they always behaved perfectly? Have we? Nowhere close. Even as I [Cheryl] write this, my husband and I continue to struggle and ache and cry because of the trials of both our kids' and our own growth. It hurts to mature. But without some pain, we wouldn't grow. Paths to understanding are often tangled and rocky, with hidden roots that trip us up. Just when we think we understand a child's stage of growth, she moves into yet another one, and we begin treading an unfamiliar trail. That's just the way life is.

When I see or hear about families who have it all together and who never seem to struggle, I know I haven't heard the whole story. Growing into our identity is a laborious process, and the contractions of delivery hurt. Fortunately, even their and our failures become part of their growth toward success. To that end my husband and I pray that in the midst of all the hubbub, our children will know Who made them and Who loves them even more than we do. A love that powerful is much harder to rebel against.

Promise Convinces

Today's self-esteem advocates are telling our children that they are wonderful. When kids believe that, they'll act differently. Won't they?

No, research tells us. Kids don't change their behavior because people say they're terrific. Descriptive adjectives like *terrific* and *wonderful* are products, results of identity, not causes of it. Kids don't believe adjectives unless they're true, unless they trust the truths they're grounded on. If behavior is going to change, we must offer children new identities that motivate them to think, speak, and act in new ways.

Let's emulate the bishop, who showed Valjean his true identity. Valjean belonged to God and was created to be loving, forgiving, strong, humble, compassionate, wise, gentle, and patient—like God is. The bishop convinced Jean Valjean of that identity by doing three things. We can follow his example in three ways.

First, we can identify and believe in the promise in a young person. The bishop saw promise in Valjean while the man was still ragged and set on thievery. As a Christian bishop, he imitated the way God reaches out to us, loving even when he was rebelled against.

Because God first loved us, we are able to love (1 John 4:19). The bishop understood this. He wasn't blind to the truth about Valjean's current state, and he understood the risks of loving him, but he saw past his temporary condition and saw his potential.

Second, we can speak nouns of promise to the young person. The bishop spoke words of promise to Valjean. He didn't use empty adjectives describing him but nouns of identity: friend, child of God. He called him "brother," elevating him to a position of equality and regard.

When we consistently tell young people that they are God's kids, his image bearers, we are setting an immutable identity before them that no failure can destroy.

Third, we can act on the young person's promise. The bishop acted unwaveringly on his belief in Valjean as God's child. Nothing Valjean did—clubbing him, stealing a fortune from him, or lying—changed the bishop's view of Valjean one iota. He sacrificed for Valjean and loved him. He challenged him to assume his newfound identity as a child of God. He showed Valjean the route to freedom from his past by showing him his identity, then standing behind him regardless of the cost.

We can do that too. We can replace labels with new identities. How? Instead of labeling Tom the alcoholic, Lucinda the tramp,

Maria the cheater, Harris the druggie, or Tamara the glutton, we can picture their promise. All of those kids are children of God, created in his likeness, who happen to be grappling with alcohol, promiscuity, dishonesty, drugs, or food. We can refuse their "permanent" labels, treating them instead as temporary problems that God's power can heal. No longer are they sentenced to those behaviors.

In their deepest being, in the DNA of every cell, in the recesses of the soul, they resemble the Lord, for whom nothing is impossible. When kids are conscious of this unchanging, exciting identity, they can't help but be motivated by it. Knowing that gives them and us hope! (Sorta makes you want to sing and dance, doesn't it?)

Remember . . .

- Motivation from identity inspires us to live as individuals created in God's image, not as people labeled by our assets or deficits.

- When kids first learn how to follow and imitate their parents, they are well on their way to learning to follow and imitate their heavenly Father, the Lord who made them.

- When we place our stamp of approval on the life of a child, the seal can last a lifetime.

- Above and beyond task mastery and the motivation it sparks, kids need a deep sense of identity to ground them, to send down roots that will keep them standing in the fiercest storms.

Chapter Ten

Integrity

*The louder he spoke of his honor, the faster we
counted our spoons.*
                              —*Ralph Waldo Emerson*

At Scimitar Ridge, an elite corporate hideaway overlooking the
San Juan Islands in Washington State, a group of Fortune 500 executives gathered for a week of accelerated leadership training. Scimitar's president, Jeff Jani, brought four teams of business leaders to a
large garage, where he gave each team a box and instructed them
to assemble a children's bicycle with the parts contained inside.
With clock-racing, competitive fervor, the teams set to work.

Meanwhile, in an adjacent room, a program assistant was helping four underprivileged eight-year-olds create thank-you cards for
the mystery gifts they were about to receive. Once the teams had
assembled the bikes, Jeff opened the garage door where those four
expectant eight-year-olds stood waiting on the other side. When
the children saw their bikes, they rushed toward them excitedly.

The executives were horrified. In their haste to win a competi-
tion, they had neglected to install brakes, tighten pedals, align han-
dlebars, and secure seats. In fact, unidentified bike parts littered the
cement floor. The bikes looked good, but *real* children couldn't ride
them!

AT-PROMISE PRINCIPLE 7: Integrity guides us to live honorably
  even when no one is looking and even when life hurts.

We Need Integrity

So far we've looked at four character traits: perseverance, responsibility for our actions, optimism, and motivation from identity. All

equip a child with tools for success. Our fifth trait, integrity, determines the quality of all other traits. Not only does integrity inspire character, but it also establishes the underpinnings of trust necessary in an At-Promise relationship.

Integrity requires us to live with our garage doors open. The executives at Scimitar were building bikes for children on the other side of the garage door. If Jeff had raised the garage door before they began assembly, their purpose would have been clear, and they would not have cut corners and compromised the integrity of their work. We can learn much from this example. In order to help children develop promise character, we need to live with transparency and consistency in both motives and behavior. What we think and do in the privacy of our own minds and homes and businesses affects those young people with whom we regularly interact.

But we need more than just transparency. We must model honorable behavior that seeks the well-being of others. When we have that selfless integrity, our children will trust us. Trust is a cornerstone of relationship. Relationship connects us to kids, so they look up to us and receive our guidance. When we have a relationship grounded on trust-building integrity, we can guide a child toward success.

Integrity Defined

Let's look at what Webster has to say about *integrity*: a state of soundness, uprightness, honesty, and sincerity.

And the dictionary only scratches the surface. Integrity is a complex trait. My [Cheryl's] ninety-two-year-old grandmother clarifies it further. She reminds me that integrity means doing what will make God smile . . .

- Whether everyone is looking or no one is
- Whether everyone will find out or no one will
- Whether it benefits me or not
- Whether it hurts or not

I believe her; she's been around a while and has earned my respect because of her own integrity. When she talks about integrity, I listen, because only with integrity can anyone truly succeed.

Practically speaking, when children develop positive values, they are better prepared for "the inevitable challenge and occasional pain of real-life decision making," says Lauro F. Cavazos, former U.S. secretary of education. Dr. Cavazos writes that "values in a school curriculum add a dimension to the benefits of academic achievement" and "provide perspective, largely by putting the individual into a community context."[1]

Garage-Door Society

But despite the need for integrity today, our culture is regularly modeling the opposite: deceit, dishonesty, betrayal, and immorality. We need look no further than recent political officeholders to see the lack of moral integrity, though we can find it in headlines about church scandals and in accounts about dishonest business dealings in some of the largest corporations in this country. Financial fraud has crippled Americans' confidence in segments of the economy, compromising investment growth and stability. CEOs of enormous corporations are being exposed as dishonorable, having scammed everyone from management to employees to investors. The public is outraged; thousands of people have lost millions of dollars through executives' fraudulent behavior.

Even so, polls conducted during political scandals invariably produce a number of comments that sound like this: "I don't care what the governor does after hours. His private life is not my business, as long as he does his job." In the face of damaging moral, financial, and political consequences, many still refuse to see the importance of personal integrity to success in society—and of a society. They like their garage doors closed.

Is it any surprise, then, that cheating is rampant in our schools? Public figures have regularly modeled cheating in business or marriage as an acceptable practice, as long as one doesn't get caught. Business leaders demonstrate that the sacrifice of integrity may be necessary in order to turn a profit.

Moral Education

Educators, equally concerned about moral decay not only among our leaders but among our young people, have made moral education a hot topic today. They are desperate for answers to the proliferation of shootings, sexual harassment, bullying, and teen promiscuity.

After wandering away from moral and character education, contemporary educators are returning to the stance of theorists like Rousseau and Dewey, who believed that the primary goal of school is to develop moral members of a free and democratic society. Horace Mann, the father of public school education in the United States, defined schools as "a moral enterprise." At the heart of that stance is the notion that "With freedom comes responsibility, but a responsibility that is based on principles that contribute to society's well-being as well as the individual's."[2]

Even in today's secular climate, noneducators and educators alike are admitting that "the challenges to our society are more than just economic or academic. Many of our problems relate to shortcomings in our morals and . . . character."[3] Despite significant theological differences, many Jews, Christians, Muslims, and various ethnic groups agree on basic principles of integrity and agree that our kids need to develop integrity's foundational traits. The issue is not whether to teach integrity but how.

Integrity in the Small Stuff

If we want children to learn integrity, then we must begin with teaching them integrity in small things of life. Day-to-day integrity translates into integrity in big issues. Consequently, our children need to practice integrity from an early age. Take honesty, for instance. Kids can't have integrity without it, but where do we draw the line between storytelling and lying in a five-year-old child?

Storytelling runs deep in my [Tim's] family. Whether it comes from my Native American heritage or simply a desire to entertain my children, I don't know. To this day, whenever my wife, Mona, runs into the store to buy a few things and I am left driving fifty times around the block, my kids inevitably ask me to tell them a story. I love every minute of it.

When they were preschoolers, we'd begin with each of them choosing to be a fictional character. (Tyler was usually some kind of raptor; Ian favored tigers or lions; and Moriah was more often than not a Bernese mountain dog.) During the course of the story, they would usually interrupt me with "Is this real, or is it a made-up story, Dad?" I could have had some fun with them and said, "No, this is a real story," but I resisted the impulse. What my children were looking for was truth. It didn't bother them if a story was made up. In fact, they were often relieved that it was, because what they really wanted to know was "Can we trust you, Dad?" For them and for all kids, fantasy and make-believe, although necessary for a well-balanced childhood, are much more fun and healthy when children know that our tales are just that: made-up stories.

I give you this illustration to make a point. It is OK for our children (and their dads) to make up tall tales, to pretend, and to create. These are natural gifts that we don't want to squelch. But just as my kids asked me, it is also OK and necessary for caring adults to ask kids the question: "Is this a made-up story?" Expecting our children to tell the truth and giving them the opportunity to tell us when they are not is a first step to developing integrity in our children.

We must insist on the same truth-telling from our older kids. Many of them learn that they can evade consequences and maneuver through life on a platform of lies. It becomes their standard way of operating. Beneath those lies is an illegitimacy, a fear of discovery that hardens conscience and makes those dodging kids harder to reach. We do young people a grave disservice when we allow them to get away with it. Surprisingly, some parents allow their children to live and speak dishonestly as long as they keep up appearances. To many that choice seems easier and more tranquil than doing battle for the sake of kids' moral fiber.

After all, truth-telling and truth-living can feel like sunbathing in a hailstorm, especially with young people! Once when I [Cheryl] was weary after yet another intense conversation with our strong-willed teenage daughter, my husband reminded me, "but she's honest, Cheryl. She wants to live with integrity. She needs to know that truth can withstand tough challenges. Be patient. She's going to be a wonderful woman." He was right. She's eighteen now, and we trust her—and have confidence in her developing character.

Life Behind the Garage Door

Taking the easy route backfires. Young people who don't develop integrity in childhood can grow into adults without integrity, as the following story illustrates.

Michelle Stephens (a pseudonym) told me [Cheryl] a story of her father, a man who believed he could separate his public and private lives. People respected and admired him. He was a leader in the church and preached principles of integrity, which he applied to many acts of public service and caregiving and verbalized energetically to his children.

But he did not live out that integrity privately. He bullied his wife and so dominated his daughter, so destroyed her "no" with his controlling behavior, that she was vulnerable to his inappropriate sexual advances toward her.

His behavior first frightened, then devastated Michelle. The absence of integrity in her father hurt her deeply and threatened to have generational impact by disconnecting and isolating her, her husband (Mike), and their children and throwing them into fear's predictably destructive pattern. Because Michelle's trust was so damaged, it took special intervention for her to begin to heal from her father's hypocrisy and abuse.

After years of denying her father's violations even to herself, Michelle confided in Anna and Don, a couple a few years older than Michelle's parents with whom the Stephenses had become friends. As Michelle gradually unfolded her story over the next few months, Anna and Don listened and supported her. Then one weekend the couple brought Michelle and her family an offer.

"My parents adopted me, so I know what it means to be 'grafted in' to a family," Don told them. "Right about now it looks like you need family. What do you think about letting Anna and me adopt you?"

God sets the lonely in families, says Psalm 68:6, just as Don and Anna set the Stephens family in theirs. They "adopted" Michelle, Mike, and their four children and offered them relationships of trust and integrity. They came alongside the family and brought the At-Promise equation to life. Over time these relationships with her new "parents" are transforming Michelle's traumatic adversity. She is learning to live with the promise character not only in her new family but in her interactions with her biological father as well.

Don and Anna have modeled promise character to the Stephenses for years now, standing with the family day in and day out, persevering in their relationships with each of them. They have shown Michelle, Mike, and their kids how truly loving people take responsibility for their actions; they have displayed optimism and hope in even the grimmest circumstances; and they have lived out their faith in God, who motivates them. They have done all of these things with integrity, both privately and publicly.

They have also done two more things in the At-Promise equation that we haven't talked about yet: Don and Anna have served others, not only the Stephens family but people in their church and community as well. And they have taken time to engage the Stephenses in play—by canoeing, celebrating holidays, and participating in other forms of joyful recreation and celebration.

These days the Stephenses are healing. Without Don and Anna's proven integrity, Michelle would never have trusted them; she and her family had been too badly injured. But for the last fifteen years, Don and Anna have loved the Stephenses well and have passed the At-Promise perspective on to two generations of their family. Instead of the oppressive denial, blame, control, and isolation in her family of origin, Michelle has joined a family that models honesty, communication, self-examination, flexibility, and hope—all in a context of integrity that allows her to trust what she is learning. And her children are being raised with At-Promise thinking.

To the individual seeking personal gain, integrity may be optional, an accessory. Success defined as heaping up wealth, fame, or power doesn't require it. But to those aspiring to contribute positively to the moral and social fabric of their communities, integrity is a nonnegotiable requirement. Living with integrity will probably cost us time, money, and ease; but without it we cannot build authentic, positive community in our families, schools, businesses, or government. Our children need us to keep our garage doors open, and then they need us to encourage them to do the same.

Remember . . .

- Integrity guides us to live honorably even when no one is looking and even when life hurts.
- When we have a relationship grounded on trust-building integrity, we can guide a child toward success.
- Living with integrity will probably cost us time, money, and ease; but without it, we cannot build authentic, positive community in our families, schools, businesses, or government.

Chapter Eleven

Service

*From now on, any definition of a successful life
must include serving others.*
—Former President George H. W. Bush

Eighteen-year-old Wayne Brisbane lives a few doors down from us [Cheryl's family]. Having shared a close friendship with the Brisbane family for years, I can accurately say that Wayne has led what many call an advantaged life, full of opportunities and love. He studies hard, runs cross-country, plays soccer, participates in student government, and is planning for college. He has good friends. His brother, sisters, parents, and extended family surround him with a network of support and encouragement. He really has all of life's perks at his disposal, as do many young people in our affluent society. But even in the midst of a setting that could keep him all too comfortable and uninterested in others' needs, Wayne has a servant's heart and has committed himself to making positive contributions to others.

Fortunately, Wayne's parents have long understood that even when a young person lives in a positive environment and enjoys caring relationships with adults, unless he experiences adversity, he will be only partially equipped to succeed in life. Now if I were a gambling woman, I'd bet my right leg that they never said to Wayne, "Well, son, if you're gonna make it in life, we've gotta make you suffer," but they have repeatedly given him chances to experience and grow through adversity. And he has.

A few months back, I asked Wayne about the time he gave to helping others and how his interest in service grew. He said this:

My parents do whatever they can for other people. Always have. I've often tagged along when they helped someone out, and at some point I began to want to help too. Once I got involved in church mission projects, I realized that what my parents had regularly said was true: "When you give, you also receive."

Last year I collected used backpacks and took them to Guatemala, where I gave them to kids who helped support their families by scavenging heaps of garbage. I had never seen anything like it before. These kids, living in the dumps . . . The whole experience stripped me. It stripped me of all the things I held on to that gave me comfort. My heart broke for them.

When I got back home, I was a different person. I'm not saying that I'm not still selfish a lot of the time, but maybe I'm just a little less focused on my own wants. Since that trip, I have started praying that God would make me a servant. I'd really like to be more like Jesus. It's funny; now whenever I feel like I want something, if I take my mind off my wants by serving people, my own needs get met, and the wants don't seem very important anymore.

Is Wayne Brisbane successful? You tell us. . . .

AT-PROMISE PRINCIPLE 8: Service humbles us by shifting our attention away from ourselves and onto the needs of others.

A Society of Self

Teaching children to think and live like servants runs counter to our culture's prevailing focus on self-promotion, self-improvement, and self-fulfillment. The latest wave of TV reality shows displays that focus all too clearly, as participants deceive, steal, cheat, manipulate, and form phony alliances in order to stay in the game. The shows attract millions of viewers, who all understand the rules of the game: success follows survival at any cost and usually at the expense of others.

Advantaged Kids Need to See Others' Needs

Unlike Wayne, our world's more advantaged children are often sheltered from need. I [Tim] remember when a prince from Saudi

Arabia brought his son, Sultan, to the private boarding school in Switzerland where Mona and I taught. That dad told me, with all sincerity, that he was excited that Sultan was finally going to discover how the rest of the world lived. I wouldn't exactly say that our $28,000-a-year school offered a true cross-sectional view of how the rest of the world lived, but it certainly differed from the boy's familiar lifestyle. When Sultan first arrived at boarding school, he assumed that the entire sixth floor would be his quarters. Imagine his shock when I showed him to his four-bunk room with a shared bathroom, one of eight such rooms on the sixth floor!

Once he settled in, I took it upon myself to give him a taste of the needs of others—through service. Every week Sultan and I collected wood in the forest for several Swiss widows who had only wood-burning stoves to heat their homes during the harsh mountain winters. I remember Sultan's pride over his first blister from hauling wood and his pleasure in providing for others. Service began opening Sultan's eyes to the needs around him. I pray that those experiences that incorporated the needs of others will have an impact on his life as a civil servant in his country.

Service Defined

Some of us have a narrow definition of service. We may limit it to hauling wood, dishing up meals at the homeless shelter, visiting shut-ins or the elderly, or signing up for a foreign mission. Service includes those acts but is so much more. Anyplace that "othering" (as my [Cheryl's] friend Donna calls it) can occur, anyplace you or I can freely forget our own wants and needs for the sake of benefiting another, is a setting for service. Richard Foster suggests that we can even and especially serve in "the tiny insignificant corners of life." We can tie a child's shoe or empty trash for a neighbor. God sees them both and thousands of simple, quiet acts just like them. Foster also identifies other types of service that gain value when they originate in a mind conformed to true, not self-inflating, service. He says that when we protect another's reputation, when we "acknowledge others and affirm their worth," when we show hospitality, listen, demonstrate empathy, and extend God's hope to one another, we are serving.[1] We can "other" like this, serve like this anywhere, when *want to* replaces *should* in our thinking. Then love, not obligation, flavors our service and directs our hands to action.

At-Promise Connection

When children serve others under the guidance of a trusted adult, they experience the interpreted adversity of the At-Promise paradigm. God-honoring service requires them to turn their focus away from themselves and toward others. That shift itself can create adversity in a young person. Involved young people regularly say that being exposed to the needs around them during a service experience was a humbling experience.

When they serve others with more serious needs, many of the kids' own complaints begin to look superficial or petty. If the young people's personal challenges are serious, service can help them see that they are not alone and that difficulty is a fact of life. And if others' pain awakens the youths to the many gifts in their own lives, they can move from a sense of entitlement to one of gratitude. Service exposes kids' priorities, as well as the extent of their compassion. That point of confrontation is often the place where character growth accelerates.

Through my [Tim's] work with young people in schools and churches, I've met lots of kids who are bent on service. They all know that my wife, Mona, and I are easy targets when it comes to supporting them. Letters and phone calls come in on a regular basis asking if we'd be willing to contribute to a trip to Haiti to work in an orphanage, a trip to Malawi to work in a refugee camp, or to a community clean-up project. I can't think of a single time when we have said no to one of those requests. Why? Because we know that serving others changes lives. By supporting kids in these service ventures, we make a small investment that yields a great reward in their lives. Talk to any kid who has gone on a service trip, and you will hear the same thing Wayne Brisbane told us: "This trip has changed me."

The At-Promise paradigm suggests that thinking of others leads to true success; selfish behavior doesn't. When New York's firefighters and police officers charged into the Twin Towers with the hope of saving lives, our country saw a crystal clear picture of what success means. Success comes through service, even at the cost of laying down one's life for another.

Kids Are Serving

Today's teens are being blasted with confusing messages about who they are and what success means. However, as we have worked closely with young people over the last few decades, we have noticed an increased awareness of social needs in school-aged children. Our observations tell us that today's kids are more involved in community service, environmental stewardship, and social justice issues than young people have been in many years. Statistics bear this out. Young people in the United States spend over 2.1 billion hours in service projects every year.[2] We encourage At-Promise mentors to nurture that interest in service, which allows kids to make genuine contributions to their communities. Those contributions are the stuff success is made of.

Young people are getting involved in their neighborhoods through service. Here's one example: for several years now, millions of kids ranging in age from college students to kindergartners have chipped in to clean up, paint, repair, and help out in countless other ways on National Youth Service Day. Projects have ranged from restoring a dilapidated playground in New Orleans to serving meals to homeless New Yorkers.[3]

Educational Research

A wonderful school movement called service learning has made significant inroads into communities by harnessing and using the teaching power of service. Service-learning programs encourage students to become active members of their communities, increase their knowledge and understanding of the communities they live in, meet real community needs, and care for others.[4]

Recent studies conducted by the Search Institute and other independent organizations have shown that students who are involved in serving others are twice as likely as children who are not involved in serving to continue serving as adults. They are more likely to vote as adults and donate a higher percentage of their income to charity. Specifically, of the students involved in service programs

- Eighty-two percent said that they would likely help a person in trouble or in need.
- Seventy-four percent were likely to change what they do in order to protect the environment.
- Seventy-two percent were likely to continue to be involved in volunteering.
- Fifty-five percent said that their service activities showed them how good it feels to help other people.
- Fifty-five percent said that their service experience showed them how much people can do when they work together as a team.[5]

Serving definitely seems to bring out the best in kids.

Modeling Service

My wife, Mona, has a wonderful way of reminding me that what I do reveals my true values. To put it bluntly, she means, "Don't tell me you value service if you are not spending time serving!" When our students and children observe us serving others, they learn that we value service.

For over a decade now, I [Tim] have taught students in a variety of settings. With each new experience come often unexpected insights. In Turkey I once grabbed a broom and started to sweep the floor after a P.E. class. Several of my senior students ran up to me in a panic and asked me to stop sweeping. It disturbed them that their teacher was doing such lowly work. I naively thought that we had reached a teachable moment about service, so I passed the broom to one of the students so that he could sweep. To my surprise he handed off the broom to an underclassman—because that made sense in his world. I was the one who learned a lesson. I learned that I needed two brooms, one for him and one for me!

Service Starts in the Home

Watching our children serve, lecturing them about serving, or financing their service is not enough. To teach service, we must sweep alongside our kids.

I [Tim] respect Sheldon Smith, a businessman, Little League baseball coach, and my dear friend and mentor. His work ethic; his leadership abilities; his love for his wife, June; and his interactions with his kids make him a person I look up to. Sheldon said this about service:

> One of the challenges today is that too many times parents get overly focused on their kids. Sometimes the roles have been reversed; parents cater to their kids, treating them as if those kids are royalty and the parents are the peasants. When I was a kid, my dad would have friends come to the house—conservation officers or other guys he would hunt with or business partners. My brothers and I would sit there and listen, but we wouldn't really be allowed to participate. If one of the boys was making too much noise, he would say "son, you're here to listen to these men, not to be talking." In our house the adults ate first. The kids served Mom and

Dad, as well as any other people who came into the house. We were taught servanthood at an early age.

That service has carried over into my home today. When we invite people into our home for a business function or whatever, my kids serve our guests. They have learned to serve at an early age just like I did. It's just natural for them. When it comes to success, work ethic, respect for adults, and service matter.

Reflection Seals the Deal

In our busy world, we set little time aside for reflection. So often we ask our kids to do something because it is the right thing to do, then fail to discuss the experience with them afterward. But if we want the right thing to have personal meaning to children (and not be just a duty that an adult assigned), we would be wise to encourage them to sit down afterward and think about the experience.

More and more research about service is telling us that children who spend time reflecting about their service experiences are more likely to see service as a personal development opportunity rather than just school work.[6] Eugene Roehlkepartain, author of *Everyone Wins When Youth Serve*, says that spending time talking and writing about a service experience is the key to gaining the most knowledge and insight from it.[7] According to the American Psychological Association's learner-centered principles, the act of thinking about the learning process (called metacognition) plays an important role in meaningful learning. One of the most powerful tools for this self-assessment process is journal writing.[8]

To employ this tool, we can encourage young people to submit simple "I Learned Statements"[9] after they serve or to write weekly journal entries focusing on their service experiences and the service needs in their community. The simple exercise of their writing down the things they learned can solidify their new insights and can give us a peek into what our children are learning. We believe that when kids reflect upon their service hours, they will take ownership of the experience. When service's value strikes them as crucial, as something they simply must do, they'll be well on their way to developing another piece of promise character.

A Servant's Heart Determines Success

We earlier defined *success* as contributing positively to the moral and social fabric of society. Inherent in that definition is the assumption that any person who wants to make such a contribution must plan on serving others. Unless we want to serve others, we will be unlikely to make the sacrifices necessary to benefit our society morally and socially.

So how can we help our children want to serve? By teaching them (through our example as well as our words) the chosen biblical mind-set that precedes and leads into meaningful service: "Do nothing out of selfish ambition or vain conceit, but in humility consider others better than yourselves. Each of you should look not only to your own interests, but also to the interests of others. Your attitude should be the same as that of Christ Jesus: Who . . . made himself nothing, taking the very nature of a servant . . . he humbled himself" (Philippians 2:3–8).

Uh-oh. Notice the imperatives in that passage? When shoulds are isolated from rewards, they don't usually motivate young people. Instead, they can act like whips on their backs, driving them into reluctant subservience, rather than physical service initiated by a willing heart and mind.

That's why we need to give kids the whole picture. We remind them of the rewards God promises when we practice those shoulds. When those reward-seeking kids hear "whoever wants to become great among you must be your servant" (Matthew 20:26), they hope for greatness. Their perseverance and optimism bloom as they anticipate those results!

Fortunately, as they seek greatness while serving, their definition of *greatness* changes. Where they may begin serving for applause and recognition, they eventually, if they stay the course, learn to serve with the true humility that God considers great. As Richard Foster explains, "Service is the most conducive to the growth of humility. When we set out on a consciously chosen course of action that accents the good of others and is for the most part a hidden work, deep change occurs in our spirit."[10] Ever so gradually, those young people can begin to see a cause and effect: in extinguishing their selfish inclinations by serving others, they can begin to find themselves!

Through this process of modeling, teaching, and letting kids practice service, we teach them how to think about service, then how to capture their thoughts and bend them into a shape compatible with serving. As they practice that attitude, their feelings will often follow, resulting in kids who want to contribute positively to their communities.

Remember . . .

- Service humbles us by shifting our attention away from ourselves and onto the needs of others.

- "It's funny; now whenever I feel like I want something, if I take my mind off my wants by serving people, my own needs get met, and the wants don't seem very important anymore."

- Anyplace that "othering" can occur, anyplace you or I can freely forget our own wants and needs for the sake of benefiting another, is a setting for service.

- When service's value strikes kids as crucial, as something they simply must do, they'll be well on their way to developing another piece of promise character.

Chapter Twelve

Engaged Play

Laughter is inner jogging.

—*Norman Cousins*

The summer after I [Cheryl] turned eight, I lived with the Siemens family. John Siemens, our family doctor, recognized the load of responsibility I felt as the eldest child in a family of rambunctious children with a depressed, overwhelmed, and angry mother. In the month after Mom moved us kids out of our grandparents' place and into town, I hadn't been eating or sleeping well. So Dr. Siemens and Mom, who really did want the best for us kids, arranged for me to spend the summer with him; his wife, Pat; and their two kids.

In a ten-minute drive across town, I went from being the big sister in a serious, chaotic, single-parent home to being the baby in a playful, peaceful family with two parents who loved each other and loved to laugh.

AT-PROMISE PRINCIPLE 9: Engaged play facilitates rest, healing, intimacy, and joy.

Play Motivates

I have remembered that summer for forty years. We gardened, played with a pet raccoon, backpacked in the Cascade and Olympic Mountains, sang dumb songs to John's ukulele, rode our bikes to Victoria, climbed through hay in Grandpa Siemens's barn, and camped on Lopez Island together.

Though I spent only three months with them, and though I was only eight years old, I returned home knowing that someday

I wanted to have a family like theirs. I had lived in their joyful home; I would remember how they lived and copy it when I grew up. Those powerful memories stuck with me. When I married and was raising a family, I often found useful family-building tools stored in my memories of the months with the Siemenses. Today I can see wonderful ways our family has resembled theirs!

A Childhood Without Play

For many North American families, *play* has become a four-letter word. University of Michigan studies showed that in 1981 children had 40 percent of their day available for free time whereas in 1997 those numbers had gone down to 25 percent. Stuart Brown, a retired psychiatrist and founder of the Institute for Play believes that "play deprivation" can lead to depression, hostility, and the loss of "things that make us human beings."[1]

According to Dr. David Elkind, author of *The Hurried Child*, parents are under more pressure than ever to overschedule their children and have them engage in organized sports and other activities that may not be age appropriate. He writes, "Divorce, single parenting, two parent working families and blended families have become the middle-class norm, and the conception of children as . . . in need of adult nurture, protection, and guidance has become a fountainhead of parental anxiety and guilt."[2]

How ironic that the childlike play we find expendable for our kids as we race them toward maturity is the very thing that they, like their parents before them, will spend so much time and energy trying to recapture when they are adults. Business consultants around the globe are making a killing by helping individuals think creatively, take risks, visualize success, collaborate, and share ideas. These characteristics of play have become essential components of achievement, both in individuals and companies. Even so, we are reluctant to allow our children much time developing those skills in play.

Play Research

There seem to be two schools of thought about children and play. On one side some researchers believe that children should start rigorous academic work at an early age so that they are more prepared to enter elementary school. Their argument is that this will close the gap between advantaged and disadvantaged children.[3]

On the other side is the belief that play is children's work and should be the primary focus of a child's life. Research supporting this view has shown that play is the best way for children to develop initiative because they are doing things that they want to do. Play is often social and is the child's first attempt at negotiations, collaboration, and relationship. It allows the child to invent, create, and determine the rules for the game. This strengthens a child's ability to self-regulate.[4]

Dr. Linda Espinosa, codirector for research and policy at the National Institution for Early Education Research at Rutgers University, suggests that play encourages children to "reflect on their own experiences through dramatization and provides an opportunity for oral language to develop."[5] This forms the basis for literacy, which in turn dramatically influences a child's ability to perform well in school.

Fearful Families Don't Play Well

Regardless of play's inherent benefits, fearful families usually don't play much. The greater the anxiety, the more serious the family. True, they may go places and participate in activities, but these are often substitutes for engaged and recreational play. Instead, the excitement of and focus on their activities serve as a distraction from their hidden fears and can actually heighten the stress of the family members, who dare not slow down enough to relax and really enjoy each another.

More often than not, when these families try to play, family members will end up isolated from one another (through an argument, misunderstanding, or mistrust), and they will either control or be controlled by each other. Knowing that once again they have failed to have fun together, they may lose hope in their family, if they haven't already. And they may try to pretend that everything is just fine.

Recreational Versus Re-Creative Play

Ask someone you know to define *playing*, and (after he squints at you and wonders why you're asking) he may toss you a list along the lines of this: competing, partying, vacationing—any kind of recreation. He might say that playing involves activities that capture attention and that can distract him from the people he's with. This sort of play focuses on the event, the game, the location, or the challenge of the play itself. Relationships are secondary to the act of recreational playing. At its most consuming, this play is exhilarating and exhausting.

Ask a second person for her definition, and she may tell you that playing is having fun with people she loves. She laughs with them, not at them. They aren't competing. Relationships are foundational to her play. She'll say that when she plays with others, they are connecting with each other—communicating, sharing, and enjoying one another's company. We like to call this kind of playing "re-creative" because those engaged in it can learn more about themselves and can come away feeling refreshed, rejuvenated, more deeply attached, and more joyful.

Engaged play fits the second definition well. Though it can take place in a recreational setting—an event like a ball game, birthday party, hike, or shopping trip—the event doesn't distract the participating people from each other. Engaged play doesn't have to be attached to an event or organized activity. It focuses on relationships, which it builds through participants' laughing, talking, listening, and enjoying each other in an atmosphere of trust that can happen anywhere. In engaged play people feel valued, safe, and respected. They can let their hair down and be vulnerable.

As John and Pat Siemens understood, engaged play shapes children in ways nothing else can. In this kind of play, adults and children can simply enjoy each other and grow more connected through positive times. We can hold memories of engaged play in reserve as fuel for hope when difficulties arise. Besides, children develop all sorts of attitudes and attributes while playing: motor skills, "initiative, self-regulation, and social skills."[6]

When we engage our children in play, its re-creative influence can be healing. It allows us all to dawdle, reflect, replenish, interact. Love-based engaged play helps us oust fear's traits of control, denial, isolation, and despair and replace them with flexibility, honesty, intimacy, and hope. Such play is necessary to our spiritual, emotional, and physical health. Of course, I didn't understand it at the time, but my stay with the Siemens family showed me just how healing such play can be.

Playing Kids Practice Success

While much of our schools' efforts to develop successful children focus on academic rigor to promote academic achievement, educators would be wise to remember that we facilitate children's success when we help them communicate effectively, make friends, solve problems, and develop a good sense of humor. Play provides a wonderful setting for developing those skills.

When children play, they don't practice failure. They practice success! In play they imagine the impossible and then accomplish it. Playing children regularly act out their dreams, giving us a window through which we can glimpse directions in which we can encourage them.

In the early 1960s, we [Cheryl's family] heated our house with wood. You know what that means: my brother, sisters, and I had a woodpile to play and dream in. I once wrote about that heap of logs.

Whenever we played with the wood, we entered an imaginary world, one in which my brother Vincent constructed mansions, using a few scraps of lumber for crossbeams and roofing, and stacked logs for walls. Inside his structure, sister Jan made grass-clipping beds for her many adopted "children." I set round logs on end—desks and stools for my "students." (I'd feed siblings and neighbors cookies if they would enroll.) My baby sister Dana decorated all our construction with fir cones and fiery red peonies that grew on a drooping bush by the smokehouse.

We didn't know it at the time, but we were all working out our dreams, practicing the blueprints God had for us. Our elders could have learned much by watching us in the woodpile. . . . Anyone observing us children with eyes for our futures would have identified my brother's love of crafting raw material into functional, beautiful objects. His hands were magic—even in the woodpile. Today he makes his living restoring antique tile roofs on historic buildings. For fun, he remodels his house and rebuilds classic cars. Sister Jan always talked of adopting children who needed homes and practiced loving them as she played in the woodpile. Today she and her husband have five adopted children, for a total of seven well-loved kids. Baby sister Dana picked bouquets everywhere, when she could. When she couldn't find flowers or cones or shells to decorate with, she made them. She is still at it, creating and selling her artwork around the state.[7]

And me? I taught young people for years. And now I write about them.

The At-Promise Connection

Engaged play fits into the At-Promise paradigm in two significant ways. First, the trusted adult in a child's life gives that child permission to be who she is: a playful child. The adult doesn't push her into an adult role but instead treasures and guards her childhood and the natural progression of growth throughout those years. She knows that play is a crucial balancing element in that growth.

Second, play affords one of the easiest ways for an adult to develop a relationship with a child. Play is therefore both a catalyst for relationship and a resulting benefit of relationship—though it can be hard on a lawn. Someday the grass in my [Tim's] yard will grow. Right now it's a muddy soccer field. On any given afternoon, Mona and I will have a half-dozen kids playing on our front yard. If you ask me to identify the biggest benefit of having been a full-time doctoral student, I will point to the time it gave me to play with my kids and their friends. Through play I have been able to love, encourage, guide, teach, and celebrate the neighborhood kids. We have gotten to know each other. Play is a bridge to relationship. Green grass can wait.

Practical Applications

Our days and nights fill up fast with duties, commitments, and work. Our minds load up with responsibilities and concerns. Adversity of one kind or another crowds our days. Sometimes we may feel that we have no time at all for the connection, rest, healing, and joy that engaged and re-creative play provide.

But we do have time. No matter what is going on, there is time to play with the children we care about. There has to be. Play balances adversity's demands; it helps keep us going. Specifically, play nourishes perseverance, buoys our optimism, and gives us a setting in which we can model responsibility for our actions, show integrity, and serve our children with love. When we play with our kids, we show them our trust that their identity, their promise is secure. Why, we can even relax and laugh with them! Dawdle awhile! Strum a ukulele! Childhood really is a blessed time given to children, and play is the path to its success.

Remember . . .

- Engaged play facilitates rest, healing, intimacy, and joy.
- How ironic that the childlike play we find expendable for our kids as we race them toward maturity is the very thing that

they, like their parents before them, will spend so much time and energy trying to recapture when they are adults.

- Engaged play doesn't have to be attached to an event or organized activity. It focuses on relationships, which it builds through participants' laughing, talking, listening, and enjoying each other in an atmosphere of trust that can happen anywhere.

- We can hold memories of engaged play in reserve as fuel for hope when difficulties arise.

Conclusion

We all know that we need more than a prescriptive formula to care for our kids. Although principles to follow, behaviors to imitate, and truths to speak are definitely helpful, we also need deep, profound hope to undergird our efforts. We need guts and hearts so sure of our children's promise that we can wait a lifetime, if necessary, without giving up on them. We need a paradigm so true that we can still trust it when all indicators tell us to accept the death of a child's promise and move on.

The At-Promise paradigm is not a formula guaranteeing that a child will choose success. It does, however, offer practical, transcending principles to help kids thrive in an at-risk world. We know that these principles can bear fruit. We've seen the results in our own lives and in the lives of our children. Wherever we—or you—have lived, At-Promise stories abound of kids who have built good character and succeeded because of an intersection of adversity and relationship. We celebrate these kids and their contributions to others!

Meanwhile other young people are waiting (though they may not know it) for trustworthy adults to enter their lives. If something has been standing between you and just such a relationship, we encourage you to walk around the barrier and begin an At-Promise friendship with a child.

Wait a minute, you think. *I have done everything this book talks about, and success is nowhere in sight. Is At-Promise thinking always true? Is the At-Promise paradigm powerful enough to bolster our friends and their jailed teenage son? Is At-Promise thinking love-filled enough to* support a student who has just been expelled from school—and who blames the system for her problems? Can At-Promise thinking sustain the hope of grief-stricken parents whose daughter has rejected their faith and turned to heroin? Will At-Promise thinking be enough for a fifteen-year-old whose father left his mother a note on the kitchen counter saying that he was leaving her and the kids?

Yes. The At-Promise paradigm is not just a human opinion or a sound theory. God, who made our kids in his likeness, declared their promise when He made them and proclaimed that promise great enough to overcome anything. David understood this when he wrote in Psalm 139:

> Oh Lord, you have searched me and you know me. . . . Where can I flee from your presence? If I go up to the heavens, you are there; if I make my bed in the depths, you are there. If I rise on the wings of the dawn, if I settle on the far side of the sea, even there your hand will guide me, your right hand will hold me fast. . . . For you created my inmost being; you knit me together in my mother's womb. . . . I am fearfully and wonderfully made.

But what about the pain? Yes, our young people will know pain, as we have. We don't know how those kids will respond to it. Nor can we control their decisions to embrace or reject their God-given promise. We can trust, however, that our loving God will not allow anything to happen that He cannot heal in one way or another. In amazing ways God offers to transmute and redeem pain and to use it to build character and ultimately success. He tells us and shows us those truths repeatedly. Our job as parents and educators is to navigate with hope as we steer our kids through whatever pain comes. We may find the wait agonizing, but we can trust God's timing. Just because healing hasn't happened when we think it should doesn't mean it won't. God has reasons for waiting, and He's not in a hurry. Essentially, Christ himself summarized the At-Promise concept when He said, "In this world you will have trouble. But take heart! I have overcome the world" (John 16:33).

The At-Promise paradigm reminds us that in often inscrutable ways, God combines adversity with trusted relationships to build promise character in our children. And the components of that character—perseverance, responsibility, optimism, motivation from identity, service, and engaged play—can lead, challenge, motivate, extrude, and invite our children into a successful life of meaningful contribution to others.

Henri J. M. Nouwen says it another way: "but in the midst of all this pain, there is a strange, shocking, yet very surprising voice. It is the voice of the one who says: 'Blessed are those who mourn: they shall be comforted.' That's the unexpected news: there is a blessing hidden in our grief. . . . Somehow, in the midst of our tears, a gift is hidden. Somehow, in the midst of our mourning, the first steps of the dance take place."[1]

At the core of our beings, we can trust God's design. We may hurt, but we don't need to be afraid for our children. Promise waits.

Study Guide: Conversation Starters

Chapter One   At Promise: A New Way of Thinking

1. Would you say that your life has been characterized more by caring relationship or more by adversity? Explain.

2. Can you identify your own At-Promise experience? Can you spot an intersection of relationship and adversity in your own life that led or can lead to growth?

Chapter Two   The At-Risk World

3. How often do you think of children as at risk? In what ways has that term limited or helped your understanding of children?

4. What risks do your children face? Specifically identify them for each child.

5. When you read that every child is at risk, how did you respond? Is it true that advantaged children are also at risk?

Chapter Three   Fear: Love's Counterfeit

6. How are your fears for your children connected to your own fears?

7. Can you recognize generational patterns of fear in your family?

8. How does fear show up in your relationships? Discuss ways the traits of control, isolation, denial, and hopelessness may influence you and those you care about.

9. Can love really overcome fear? Why or why not? Include the traits of flexibility, connectedness, honesty, and hope in your discussion.

Chapter Four   Adversity and Pain Can Lead to Growth

10. Is adversity essential to growth? Why or why not?

11. How has adversity influenced you? Your relationships? Your choices?

12. How has a relationship helped you interpret your pain?

Chapter Five   Trust Between a Caring Adult and a Child

13. Describe key individuals in your life. How did they influence you?

14. Which child in your life do you see as At Promise?

15. What steps are you taking (or willing to take) to deliberately build relationship with that child?

16. How often do you evaluate the benefit of a program for your child based on its convenience? On its potential for positive relationships?

17. Describe your relationship with God. How does that relationship influence you—how you see yourself, your trials, your children?

Chapter Six   Perseverance

18. Have you given your child opportunities to struggle? Describe them. Are you glad you did?

19. Romans 5:3–5 says that we are to "rejoice in our sufferings, because we know that suffering produces perseverance; perseverance, character; and character, hope. And hope does not . . . disappoint us." Has this been true in your life? Discuss.

20. Can a person succeed without having perseverance?

21. How does faith affect perseverance?

Chapter Seven   Responsibility for Our Actions

22. Discuss this statement: "Helpless people blame others."

23. How do we decide when to show our children grace and when to apply consequences? How do we balance the two?

24. Do your children tend to believe they have lots of options or very few? Explain.

25. Can you identify a time when you had to take responsibility for your own actions? How did that experience affect you?

Chapter Eight   Optimism

26. Do you believe we can change our feelings by changing our thoughts? Discuss.

27. Do you honestly have hope for your children? For some more than others? Explain.

28. Do you consider self-esteem important? Why or why not? Has the book's discussion influenced your opinion?

29. Think of the most optimistic person you know. What can you learn from that person?

Chapter Nine   Motivation from Identity

30. Who are you? What motivates you?

31. How does your conditional identity motivate your behavior and your choices? Your unconditional identity? Give examples.

32. What are you doing to help your kids understand their identity?

33. How does your children's identity influence their behavior and choices?

Chapter Ten   Integrity

34. Describe a situation in which you have had to choose between right and wrong. How did you choose? Why?

35. How do you encourage children to tell the truth? Have you been successful? Why or why not?

36. What are the ingredients of integrity? Are they all equally important?

37. What does it mean to live with your garage doors open?

Chapter Eleven   Service

38. What role does serving others play in your life? In your thinking? In your actions?

39. What are practical ways you can expose your children to the needs of others?

40. How does service contribute to success?

41. What does the term *servant leadership* mean to you?

Chapter Twelve   Engaged Play

42. Do you play with your children? Is your play recreational or re-creative?

43. How do you respond to this line: "There is always time to play"?

44. How does fear keep our children and us from engaged play?

45. What role does play have in success?

Comprehensive Questions

46. What is the most difficult aspect of the At-Promise paradigm for you to accept? Why?

47. What aspect of the At-Promise paradigm offers you the most hope? Why?

Notes

Introduction

1. B. B. Swadener and S. Lubeck (eds.), *Children and Families "At Promise": Deconstructing the Discourse of Risk* (Albany: State University of New York Press, 1995).

Chapter One   At Promise: A New Way of Thinking

1. A. Holmes, "Foreword to the Proceedings from the First National Symposium for Nurturing Reflective Christian Teachers." In D. Elliott (ed.), *Nurturing Reflective Christians to Teach: A Valiant Role for the Nation's Christian Colleges and Universities* (Lanham, N.Y.: University Press of America, 1995).
2. L. Calhoun and R. Tedeschi, "Beyond Recovery from Trauma: Implications for Clinical Practice and Research," *Journal of Social Issues*, 1998, 54(2), 357–371.
3. M. Seligman, *The Optimistic Child: A Proven Program to Safeguard Children Against Depression and Build Lifelong Resilience* (New York: Houghton Mifflin, 1995).

Chapter Two   The At-Risk World

1. A. C. Ornstein and F. P. Hunkins, *Curriculum: Foundations, Principles, and Issues*, 3rd ed. (Boston: Allyn & Bacon, 1998).
2. Child Welfare League of America, "National Fact Sheet, 2001," http://www.cwal.org/advocacy/nationalfactsheet00.htm, 2002.

3. Advocates for Youth, "Adolescent Pregnancy and Childbearing," http://www.advocatesforyouth.org/publications/factsheet/fsprechd.htm, February 7, 2003.

4. Z. Breznitz and G. Norman, "Differences in Concentration Ability Among Low- and High-SES Israeli students: A Follow-Up Study." *Journal of Genetic Psychology*, 1998, *159*, 82–84.

5. C. Edwards, "Grade Inflation: The Effects on Educational Quality and Personal Well-Being." *Education*, 2000, *120*, 538–547.

6. J. A. Banks and C.A.M. Banks (eds.), *Multicultural Education: Issues and Perspectives*, 4th ed. (New York: Wiley, 2001).

7. J. Galbo, "Adolescents' Perceptions of Significant Adults," *Adolescence*, 1983, *18*, 417–427.

8. A. Lamott, *Bird by Bird: Some Instructions on Writing and Life* (New York: Anchor Books, 1994).

Chapter Four   *Adversity and Pain Can Lead to Growth*

1. A. Desetta and S. Wolin (eds.), *The Struggle to Be Strong: True Stories by Teens About Overcoming Tough Times* (Minneapolis: Free Spirit, 2000).

2. M. Rutter, "Psychosocial Adversity: Risk, Resilience, and Recovery," *Southern Africa Journal of Child and Adolescent Psychiatry*, 1995, *7*, 75–88.

3. E. E. Werner and R. S. Smith, *Overcoming the Odds: High-Risk Children from Birth to Adulthood* (Ithaca, N.Y.: Cornell University Press, 1992).

4. M. C. Snape, "Reactions to Traumatic Events: The Good, the Bad, and the Ugly?" *Psychology, Health, and Medicine*, 1997, *2*(3), 237–242.

5. J. H. McMillan and D. F. Reed, "At-Risk Students and Resiliency: Factors Contributing to Academic Success." *Clearing House*, 1994, *67*(3), 137–143.

6. V. Goertzel and M. Goertzel, *Cradles of Eminence* (New York: Little, Brown, 1962).

7. E. Woods, *Training a Tiger* (New York: HarperCollins, 1997).
8. N. M. Lambert and B. L. McCombs (eds.), *How Students Learn: Reforming Schools Through Learner-Centered Education* (Washington, D.C.: American Psychological Association, 1998).
9. A. Ellis, *Research on Educational Innovations*, 3rd ed. (Larchmont, N.Y.: Eye on Education, 2001).
10. R. F. Baumeister, L. Smart, and J. M. Boden, "Relation of Threatened Egotism to Violence and Aggression: The Dark Side of High Self-Esteem." *Psychological Review*, 1996, *103*(1), 5–33.
11. Lamott, *Bird by Bird*.

Chapter Five   Trust Between a Caring Adult and a Child

1. Holmes, "Foreword."
2. Werner and S. Smith, *Overcoming the Odds*.
3. T. M. Levy and M. Orlans, *Attachment, Trauma, and Healing: Understanding and Treating Attachment Disorder in Children and Families* (Washington, D.C.: Child Welfare League of America, 1998).
4. P. L. Benson, P. Scales, N. Leffert, and E. Roehlkepartain, *A Fragile Foundation: The State of Developmental Assets Among American Youth* (Minneapolis: Search Institute, 1999).
5. M. Fraser, *Risk and Resilience in Childhood: An Ecological Perspective* (Washington, D.C.: NASW Press, 1997).
6. Benson and others, *A Fragile Foundation*.
7. J. Galbo, "Adolescents' Perceptions of Significant Adults."
8. Ibid.
9. R. Nydam, "How Do People Change?" *Calvin Theological Seminary Forum*, 2002, *9*(2), 12.

Chapter Six   Perseverance

1. Americans for Divorce Reform, "Divorce Rates," http://www.divorcereform.org/rates.html, July 2002.

2. National Institute of Mental Health, "Suicide Facts," http://www.nimh.nih.gov/research/suifact.htm, March 2002.
3. National Center for Education Statistics, "Dropout Rates," http://www.nces.ed.gov/pubs2002/2002022.pdf, November 2000.
4. M. Seligman, *Learned Optimism: How to Change Your Mind and Your Life* (New York: Pocket Books, 1998).
5. J. Bufill, "An Assisted Suicide Kills More Than One Victim," *USA Today*, June 4, 2002, p. 13A.

Chapter Seven   *Responsibility for Our Actions*

1. Seligman, *Learned Optimism*.
2. U.S. Department of Justice, "American Indians and Crime," http://www.ojp.usdoj.gov/bjs/pub/press/aic.pr, February 14, 1999.
3. M. Gredler, *Learning and Instruction: Theory into Practice*, 4th ed. (Upper Saddle River, N.J.: Prentice Hall, 2001).
4. J. McMahon, F. McMahon, and T. Romano, *Psychology and You*, 2nd ed. (Saint Paul, Minn.: West, 1995).
5. Ibid.
6. E. Peterson, *The Message* (Colorado Springs, Colo.: NavPress, 1995).

Chapter Eight   *Optimism*

1. M. Seligman, *The Optimistic Child: A Proven Program to Safeguard Children Against Depression and Build Lifelong Resilience* (New York: HarperCollins, 1995).
2. Gredler, *Learning and Instruction*.
3. Ellis, *Research on Educational Innovations*.
4. Seligman, *Optimistic Child*.
5. Ibid.

Chapter Nine   *Motivation from Identity*

1. B. August (dir.), *Les Miserables* [motion picture] (Los Angeles: TriStar, 1998).

2. Quoted in C. J. Sommerville, *The Rise and Fall of Childhood* (New York: Vintage Books, 1990).

3. N. M. Lambert and B. L. McCombs (eds.), *How Students Learn: Reforming Schools Through Learner-Centered Education* (Washington, D.C.: American Psychological Association, 1998).

Chapter Ten   Integrity

1. L. Cavazos, "Emphasizing Performance Goals and High-Quality Education for All Students." *Phi Delta Kappan*, 2002, 83(9), 690–718.

2. J. Fraser, *Between Church and State: Religion and Public Education in a Multicultural America* (New York: St. Martin's Press, 1999).

3. A. C. Ornstein and F. P. Hunkins, *Curriculum: Foundations, Principles, and Issues*, 3rd ed. (Boston: Allyn & Bacon, 1998).

Chapter Eleven   Service

1. R. Foster, *Celebration of Discipline* (San Francisco: HarperSanFrancisco, 1978).

2. J. Griffin-Wiesner, "Youth See Benefits of Serving Others," *Youth Update Newsletter*, http://www.search-institute.org/archives/ysboso.htm, May 1995.

3. Ibid.

4. S. Billig, "Research on K–12 School-Based Service-Learning: The Evidence Builds," *Phi Delta Kappan*, 2000, 81, 658–664.

5. Griffin-Wiesner, "Youth See Benefits."

6. P. Scales and others, "The Effects of Service-Learning on Middle School Students' Social Responsibility and Academic Success," *Journal of Early Adolescence*, 2000, 20, 332–359.

7. Griffin-Wiesner, "Youth See Benefits."

8. Lambert and McCombs, *How Students Learn*.

9. A. Ellis, *Teaching, Learning, and Assessment Together: The Reflective Classroom* (Larchmont, N.Y.: Eye on Education, 2001).

10. Foster, *Celebration of Discipline*.

Chapter Twelve   Engaged Play

1. W. Kirn, "Whatever Happened to Play?" *Time*, April 30, 2001, pp. 56–58.
2. D. Elkind, *The Hurried Child: Growing Up Too Fast, Too Soon*, 3rd ed. (Cambridge, Mass.: Perseus, 2001).
3. E. D. Hirsch Jr., *The Schools We Need and Why We Don't Have Them* (New York: Doubleday, 1996).
4. S. Hofferth and J. Sandberg, "How American Children Spend Their Time," *Journal of Marriage and the Family*, 2001, 63(2), 285–309.
5. L. Espinosa, "Set the Stage for Literacy—Literally: A Trusting Relationship and Plenty of Play Time Lay the Foundation for Successful Readers," *Scholastic Parent and Child*, October 2002, p. 36.
6. Hofferth and Sandberg, "How American Children Spend Their Time."
7. C. Bostrom, *The View from Goose Ridge: Watching Nature, Seeing Life* (Nashville: Nelson, 2001).

Conclusion

1. H.J.M. Nouwen, *With Burning Hearts* (Maryknoll, N.Y.: Orbis Books, 1994).

Recommended Reading

Abbott, D., and Meredith, W. "The Influence of a Big Brothers Program on the Adjustment of Boys in Single-Parent Families." *Journal of Psychology*, 1997, *131*, 143–157.

Affleck, G., and Tennen, H. "Constructing Benefits from Adversity: Adaptational Significance and Dispositional Underpinnings." *Journal of Personality*, 1996, *64*, 899–922.

Affleck, G., and others. "Causal Attribution, Perceived Benefits, and Morbidity Following a Heart Attack." *Journal of Consultation and Clinical Psychology*, 1987, *55*, 29–35.

Bandura, A. *Social Learning Theory*. Upper Saddle River, N.J.: Prentice-Hall, 1977.

Bandura, A., and Walters, R. *Social Learning and Personality Development*. Austin, Tex.: Holt, Rinehart and Winston, 1963.

Beitchman, J. H., and others. "A Review of the Long-Term Effects of Child Sexual Abuse." *Child Abuse and Neglect*, 1992, *16*, 101–118.

Benson, P., and others. *A Fragile Foundation: The State of Developmental Assets Among American Youth*. Minneapolis: Search Institute, 1999.

Bernard, B. *Fostering Resiliency in Kids: Protective Factors in Family, School, and Community*. Portland, Ore.: Western Center for Drug-Free Schools and Communities, 1991.

Bernard, B. *Fostering Resilience in Children*. Urbana, Ill.: ERIC Clearinghouse on Elementary and Early Childhood Education, 1995.

Collins, P. "Does Mentorship Among Social Workers Make a Difference? An Empirical Investigation of Career Outcomes." *Social Work*, 1994, *39*, 413–420.

Davidson, W. S., and Redner, R. "The Prevention of Juvenile Delinquency: Diversion from the Juvenile Justice System." In R. H. Price and others (eds.), *Fourteen Ounces of Prevention: Theory, Research, and Prevention*. New York: Pergamon Press, 1988.

Du Bois, D. L., and Neville, H. A. "Youth Mentoring: Investigation of Relationship Characteristics and Perceived Benefits." *Journal of Community Psychology*, 1997, *25*, 227–234.

Flynn, L. "The Adolescent Parenting Program: Improving Outcomes Through Mentorship." *Public Health Nursing*, 1999, *16*, 182–190.

Gall, M., Borg, W., and Gall, J. *Educational Research: An Introduction.* (6th ed.) New York: Longman, 1996.

Garmezy, N. "Stress-Resistant Children: The Search for Protective Factors." In J. E. Stevenson (ed.), *Recent Research in Developmental Psychopathology (Journal of Child Psychology and Psychiatry Book Suppl. 4).* Oxford: Pergamon Press, 1985.

Garmezy, N. "Stress, Competence, and Development: Continuities in the Study of Schizophrenic Adults, Children Vulnerable to Psychopathology, and the Search for Stress-Resistant Children." *American Journal of Orthopsychiatry*, 1987, *57*, 159–174.

Garmezy, N. "Resiliency and Vulnerability to Adverse Developmental Outcomes with Poverty." *American Behavioral Scientist*, 1991, *34*, 416–431.

Green, S. B., and others. *Using SPSS for Windows: Analyzing and Understanding Data.* (2nd ed.) Upper Saddle River, N.J.: Prentice Hall, 2000.

Howard, S. "What Makes the Differences? Children and Teachers Talk About Resilient Outcomes for Children 'At Risk.'" *Educational Studies*, 2000, *26*, 321–339.

Howard, S., and Dryden, J. (1999). Childhood Resilience: Review and Critique of the Literature." *Oxford Review of Education*, 1999, *25*, 307–313.

Husted, S. W. "The Role of Challenge as a Motivating Force in Academic Engagement for At-Risk Youth: Outward Bound Revisited." *Dissertation Abstracts International*, 1999, *60*(1A), 58.

Kendall-Tackett, K. A., and others. "Impact of Sexual Abuse on Children: A Review and Synthesis of Recent Empirical Studies." *Psychological Bulletin*, 1993, *113*, 164–180.

Leffert, N., and others. "Developmental Assets: Measurement and the Prediction of Risk Behaviors Among Adolescents." *Applied Developmental Science*, 1998, *2*, 209–230.

Lehman, D., and others. "Positive and Negative Life Changes Following Bereavement and Their Relations to Adjustment." *Journal of Social and Clinical Psychology*, 1993, *12*, 90–112.

Licht, M. "Multiple Regression and Correlation." In L. Grimm and P. Yarnold (eds.), *Reading and Understanding Multivariate Statistics.* Washington, D.C.: American Psychological Association, 1995.

McMillen, J. C. "Better for It: How People Benefit from Adversity." *Social Work*, 1999, *44*(5), 1–16.

McMillen, J. C., Zuravin, S., and Rideout, G. B. "Perceptions of Benefit from Child Sexual Abuse." *Journal of Consulting and Clinical Psychology*, 1995, *63*, 1037–1043.

National Commission on Excellence in Education. *A Nation at Risk: The Imperative for Educational Reform.* Washington, D.C.: National Commission on Excellence in Education, 1983.

Nettles, S. M. "Understanding Resilience: The Role of Social Resources." *Journal of Education of Students Placed at Risk*, 2000, 5, 47–69.

Pann, J. M. "The Effects of an Adventure Education Intervention of Self-Concept and Verbal Academic Achievement in Inner-City Adolescents." *Dissertation Abstracts International*, 2000, 60(10-A), 3606.

Reed, D. F., and others. "Defying the Odds: Middle Schoolers in High-Risk Circumstances Who Succeed." *Middle School Journal*, 1995, 27, 3–10.

Rhodes, J. E., and others. "The Influence of Mentoring on Peer Relationships of Foster Youth in Relative and Non-Relative Care." *Journal of Research on Adolescence*, 1999, 9, 185–202.

Rutter, M. "Psychosocial Resilience and Protective Mechanisms." In J. Rolf and others (eds.), *Risk and Protective Factors in the Development of Psychopathology*. New York: Cambridge University Press, 1990.

Scales, P. "The Role of Family Support Programs in Building Developmental Assets Among Young Adolescents: A National Survey of Services and Staff Training Needs." *Child Welfare*, 1997, 76, 611–636.

Scales, P. "Reducing Risks and Building Developmental Assets: Essential Actions for Promoting Adolescents' Health." *Journal of School Health*, 1999, 69, 113–120.

Scales, P., and others. "Contribution of Developmental Assets to the Prediction of Thriving Among Adolescents." *Applied Developmental Science*, 2000, 20, 332–359.

Schissel, B. "Coping with Adversity: Testing the Origins of Resiliency in Mental Health." *International Journal of Social Psychiatry*, 1993, 39, 34–46.

Slicker, E. K., and Palmer, D. J. "Mentoring At-Risk High School Students: Evaluation of a School-Based Program." *School Counselor*, 1993, 40, 327–334.

Torrance, E. "Role of Mentors in Creative Achievement." *Creative Child and Adult Quarterly*, 1983, 8, 8–15.

Vogt, W. P. *Dictionary of Statistics and Methodology: A Nontechnical Guide for the Social Sciences*. (2nd ed.) Thousand Oaks, Calif.: Sage, 1999.

Weiss, T. *Posttraumatic Growth in Husbands of Women with Breast Cancer*. Doctoral dissertation, Adelphi University, 2000.

Werner, E. E. "Research in Review: Resilient Children." *Young Children*, 1984, 40, 68–72.

Werner, E. E., and Smith S. *Vulnerable but Invincible: A Longitudinal Study of Resilient Children and Youth*. New York: McGraw-Hill, 1982.

The Authors

Timothy S. Stuart, Ed.D., serves as the high school principal at Rehoboth Christian School in New Mexico. He is a Gates Millennium Scholar and founder and president of At Promise, Inc. A member of North Carolina's High Plains Saponny Indian tribe, he is former associate director of Washington State University's Native Teacher Preparation Program at NW Indian College. He has also served as a secondary teacher and coach. He and his wife, Mona, have been married for eight years and have three children.

Cheryl G. Bostrom, M.A., a former Teacher of the Year, has taught and mentored junior and senior high school students in both public and private Christian schools. She is an inspirational retreat and conference speaker, and former feature columnist for Women of Faith.com. Her previous book, *The View from Goose Ridge*, was published by Thomas Nelson in 2001. She and her husband, Blake, have been married for twenty-seven years. They have a grown son and daughter.